Dear Reader:

The book you a[...]
Martin's True C[...]
"the leader in tr[...]
account of the latest, most sensational crime that has captured the
national attention. St. Martin's is the publisher of bestselling true
crime author and crime journalist Kieran Crowley, who explores
the dark, deadly links between a prominent Manhattan surgeon and
the disappearance of his wife fifteen years earlier in THE SUR-
GEON'S WIFE. Suzy Spencer's BREAKING POINT guides readers
through the tortuous twists and turns in the case of Andrea Yates,
the Houston mother who drowned her five young children in the
family's bathtub. In Edgar Award-nominated DARK DREAMS, leg-
endary FBI profiler Roy Hazelwood and bestselling crime author
Stephen G. Michaud shine light on the inner workings of America's
most violent and depraved murderers. In the book you now hold,
BABY BE MINE, Edgar Award nominee Diane Fanning tells the tragic tale of the murder of a pregnant Missouri woman . . . allegedly by
a woman who wanted her baby.

St. Martin's True Crime Library gives you the stories behind the
headlines. Our authors take you right to the scene of the crime and
into the minds of the most notorious murderers to show you what
really makes them tick. St. Martin's True Crime Library paperbacks are better than the most terrifying thriller, because it's all
true! The next time you want a crackling good read, make sure it's
got the St. Martin's True Crime Library logo on the spine—you'll
be up all night!

Charles E. Spicer, Jr.
Executive Editor, St. Martin's True Crime Library

BABY BE MINE

The Shocking True Story of a Woman Accused
of Murdering a Pregnant Woman to Steal Her Child

DIANE FANNING

St. Martin's Paperbacks

BABY BE MINE

Copyright © 2006 by Diane Fanning.

Cover photo of Lisa Montgomery courtesy AP/Wide World Photos. Photo of Bobbie Jo Stinnett by Zuma/courtesy of Nodaway-Holt High School.

All rights reserved. No part of this book may be used or reproduced in any manner whatsoever without written permission except in the case of brief quotations embodied in critical articles or reviews. For information address St. Martin's Press, 175 Fifth Avenue, New York, NY 10016.

ISBN: 0-312-93873-X
EAN: 9780312-93873-4

Printed in the United States of America

St. Martin's Paperbacks edition / September 2006

St. Martin's Paperbacks are published by St. Martin's Press, 175 Fifth Avenue, New York, NY 10010.

10 9 8 7 6 5 4 3 2 1

This book is dedicated to the memory of Bobbie Jo Stinnett
And to the beautiful daughter she left behind.

Acknowledgments

I t is hard to know where to begin when you have so many people to thank. So, I'll just start at the point where my research began—the St. Joseph Police Department— thanks to Chief Mike Hirter, Commander Larry Smith, Sergeant Mike Wilson and Sergeant Curtis Howard, and to retired St. Joseph's Police Chief Lloyd Pasley.

Thanks to Nodaway County Sheriff Ben Espey for his time and for the determined commitment he brought to Bobbie Jo Stinnett's case, and to Detective Randy Strong of the Maryville Public Safety Department, Sergeant Dave Merrill of the Missouri Highway Patrol and Osage County Sheriff Laurie Dunn.

No true crime writer can ever express enough appreciation to the folks who work in district and circuit court clerks' offices in counties coast to coast. Their help is of immeasurable value. This time around, I owe a debt of gratitude to Curtis

Quick of Calloway County, Vicki Mills of Franklin County, Rita Stevens of Atchison County and the staff in the court clerks' offices in Osage County, Boone County and Nodaway County.

I also need to thank the folks in the office of U.S. Representative Sam Graves for their assistance and acknowledge the Court TV Crime Files for background on Ken McElroy. Thanks, too, to Lydia Tederick, Assistant Curator at the White House and Don Ledford in the public affairs division of the Office of the United States Attorney for the Western District of Missouri.

In Kansas, I want to express my appreciation to Isabel Phelon, Kathy Dewey and Judy Shaughnessy. To Darrell Schultze—thanks for sharing the warmth of your wood stove and your personality on a cold November evening. In Missouri, a big thank you to Becky Harper, Cheryl Huston, Carla Wetzel, Mary Rose Wiederholtz, psychic Joyce Morgan, Chuck Ellis and Will and Donna Mae Schneider. In both states, thanks to all the folks who shared their thoughts and memories but requested anonymity.

In the world of rat terrier aficionados, I must point out the great people I met there: Jason Dawson, Dyanne Siktar and Pat Kennedy.

I extend very special, heartfelt thanks to Northwest Missouri native Teri McCarthy of McCarthy Print in Austin and to all the gang at PPSD for helping me to make important connections. And to Lysa M. Nistico, John Pinter, and Jennifer Steves—thanks for your help.

To Cathy Nahirny, John Rabun and Stephanie Rodriquez at the National Center for Missing and Exploited Children, thank you for your input and assistance. To the three of you and to all of the dedicated people of your organization, thank you for all the hard work you do for children and families. Because of your efforts, the world is a better place.

As always, there are a few people I need to thank with

every book I write: my peerless agent Jane Dystel, St. Martin's Press executive editor, Charlie Spicer, and my ever-patient editor Joe Cleemann. And finally, the priceless support of my first reader, best friend and life partner, Wayne.

1

Chris Law looked out the window of his home onto Elm Street, a quiet neighborhood in the small run-down town of Skidmore in the northwest corner of Missouri. Most of the houses on that dead end street cried out for a fresh coat of paint or the immediate attention of a carpenter or roofer. They huddled together tired and neglected—sagging beneath the weight of a cold December day. The bare branches of the trees and the winter weariness of the lawns added to the bleakness of the block.

Chris peered catty-corner across the street to the little white bungalow with flaking paint that Zeb and Bobbie Jo Stinnett called home. They were a cute couple—friendly but quiet. Bobbie Jo, though, had a sparkle in her eye that revealed an ornery sense of humor beneath her gentle, still demeanor.

The young couple in their early twenties were newlyweds—their marriage less than two years old. They were already expecting their first child—the due date was

January 19. The coming of the baby created a growing excitement for their tomorrows. They saved every penny they could to build a nest egg and make it possible to own their own home. They envisioned a life for their baby that exceeded the expectations they had for their own.

Now just nine days before Christmas, Bobbie Jo had reached that awkward, waddling stage. She rolled up the sidewalk more than she walked. She had to hold on to a secure object when she bent down to pick something up off the floor.

Chris had planned to walk over and pay a visit to Bobbie Jo that afternoon. He wanted to ask her about her recent prenatal test results. In a town this small, everyone focused on each expectant mother. With the population shrinking, any birth was big news.

He hesitated when he spotted a dirty, pinkish-red two-door import parked the wrong way in front of her house. He thought he ought not to bother Bobbie Jo, since she had company. He popped his head up to the window a couple of times to see if the coast was clear so he could slip over without interrupting her social visit.

It seemed to him as if the car was there for hours. But he could have been wrong. Waiting for a change of events over which he had no control did make time crawl slower than the sand in a clogged hourglass.

Sometime well before 3:30, he decided he would catch up with Bobbie Jo later. He jumped in his car to drive the fourteen miles up State Road V to Maryville to run a few errands. His town had no grocery store, pharmacy, fast food restaurants or even a Wal-Mart.

As he hit the end of Elm Street, he had second thoughts—maybe he should stop in and check on Bobbie Jo anyway. What if something was wrong? He pulled out on the main road and circled around a block as he toyed with the idea. Ultimately, he decided not to yield to his sudden flash of paranoia. He'd be a good neighbor and not disrupt her visit with her guests. He headed on up the road.

Once Chris left home, no one was watching 410 Elm Street.

Bobbie Jo was alone with her mystery visitor. The rat terriers she bred out of her huge love of animals and passion for the breed—and for a small profit—were put up in their room. No neighbor looked as the front door jerked all the way open. Not a soul saw the dirty-blond woman with the frenzied eyes and furtive moves walk across the front porch. No one took note of the blanketed bundle cradled in her arms. No one watched as she scurried to her car, pulling the bundle closer to her chest as if sheltering it from the wind and the cold. No one heard the unmistakable cry of a newborn infant. No eyes followed the dirty red car with Kansas plates as it made a rough U-turn at the dead end of Elm Street and drove off to parts unknown.

A short while later, Becky Harper turned onto Elm Street. She passed the big yellow house with its toy-laden porch and splotchy lawn. She drove beyond a sad, sagging home with a weedy front yard. She turned around at the dead end and pulled in front of her daughter Bobbie Jo's home. It was 3:30 in the afternoon.

The front door to the tiny bungalow was ajar. A tingle of concern sent ripples across her scalp. Folks in Northwest Missouri simply did not leave their doors open to the cold of December. Even nice sunny days bore too much chill in the air.

Becky pushed the door all the way open, hollering, "Bobbie Jo! Bobbie Jo!"

There was no response. A tight band of apprehension tugged in her chest. Bobbie Jo was eight months pregnant. Had she gone into early labor? Was she sick—too sick to respond? Becky hesitated with each step she took into the house.

Stepping inside the home, she saw nothing to cause alarm. Everything was neat and orderly in the living room. She moved to the dining room and the kitchen. Everything was in its place. Even this late in her pregnancy, Bobbie Jo maintained the tidy appearance of her modest home. Becky called out to her daughter again and was greeted by frustrated barks from Bobbie Jo's dogs. Becky moved past the kitchen and toward the animals confined in the small bedroom Bobbie Jo transformed into a room for her dogs. Barks and whimpers emerged from the metal kennel cages lining the room. Against one wall, an old dresser served as a grooming station for her rat terriers.

As she reached the doorway, a vision out of a slaughterhouse exploded before Becky's eyes. Blood. Pools of blood. Garish red smears streaked and swirled on the oak floor boards. Huge, dark clots of blood scattered on the surface like trampled roses in mud.

Becky saw the body on the floor, but in her heart she wanted to believe all this carnage was from one of the dogs. Whatever horrible thing happened to any one of them would break Bobbie Jo's heart. She could deny the reality before her dazed eyes for brief seconds only. There at her feet lay her only daughter—the mother of her soon-to-be first grandchild—and she was covered in blood. The young woman who, twenty-three short years ago, was only a small warm burden inside of Becky's body now lay still on the floor.

Splotches of blood covered Bobbie Jo's face. Streaks of ruby red ran up and down her arms. Her belly, distended from pregnancy, splayed open to reveal protruding internal organs scorched with a screaming crimson. Even the small soles of Bobbie Jo's feet glistened with blood.

Becky's eyes saw the truth of the horror. Her mind ran from it. Her eyes had to be lying. She tried to deny the truth of her senses and failed. Still, the scene made no sense to her. She struggled to frame it into a coherent possibility. "My daughter's intestines exploded," she said when she called 9-1-1.

As soon as the words passed her lips, she was no longer certain of their reliability. Her world tilted and wobbled on an unreliable axis. She was undone.

The operator asked, "Is she still breathing?"

"I don't know," Becky wailed. She kneeled in the blood

beside her oldest child's side struggling to numb the paralyzing emotions that siezed her own limbs. She followed instructions as the operator talked her step-by-step through the administration of cardio-pulmonary resuscitation.

She tilted back Bobbie Jo's head and pinched her nose. She covered her daughter's mouth with her own and delivered the sharpest breath she could. She rose up and placed her hands on Bobbie Jo's chest and pushed down. One time. Two times. Thirty times.

In less than twenty seconds she was back on her daughter's mouth with two more breaths. Then back to the chest compressions again. Over and over. Breathing and pushing. Counting the compressions aloud to block the noise of her own dreadful thoughts and keep her focus.

She choked. She sobbed. But she did not stop.

Four-term Nodaway County Sheriff Ben Espey was in the dispatch center in Maryville when Becky's frantic call shattered the peace of a quiet afternoon. He jumped in his truck and floored the pedal—making the half-hour drive in fourteen minutes. He was the first responder on the scene.

Becky turned to him with crazed yet determined eyes and pleaded, "I need help with this." CPR was so simple but so exhausting.

Espey got down on the floor to assist. He smelled the slight musky undertone of dog present even in this clean, well-kept kennel. Blaring above that scent was the iron-rich scream of freshly-shed blood. He saw no signs of life in the body of the young woman on the floor, but did not whisper his fears to the mother. He just worked with Becky as a team while distressed dogs whimpered their mournful fears.

On the east end of Elm Street, Carla Wetzel heard the howl of the sirens. She could not see where the vehicles stopped. But it was just past the time school let out and she worried that a school bus had wrecked.

Across the street from the Stinnett home, Tracy Grossoehme played in the yard with her two small children, enjoying the relative balminess of that winter afternoon. They stopped what they were doing as the ambulance pulled into their street, staring open-mouthed.

As it parked in front of their neighbor's home, Tracy's oldest child asked, "Can we say a prayer for the hurt person?"

"Yes, we can," Tracy said.

Three heads bowed in a moment of silence, marking the first public prayer sent to the heavens for Bobbie Jo and her baby. It certainly would not be the last.

Five minutes after Espey's arrival, the paramedics flew out of the ambulance and into the house, where they relieved Becky and the sheriff of their hopeless duty. The emergency medical pair checked for vital signs and found no indication of life. Just the same, they attempted to revive Bobbie Jo, continuing the performance of CPR her mother started, but they, too, failed to get a response. It was far too late.

Espey told the paramedics that Bobbie Jo was eight months pregnant. He then listened in disbelief as one of the emergency medical technicians pointed to the cut umbilical cord and informed him, "This lady has been murdered because someone came to get the child out of her body."

It didn't seem possible. Espey struggled to wrap his mind around the crime. How could anyone attack a pregnant woman? How could anyone abduct a baby in such a vicious, violent way? In his mind, he ran through the list of brutal people in his jurisdiction. Certainly there were those who could commit murder. But someone who would kill this young woman and then run off with the baby? It made no sense.

In the kitchen, the shell of Becky Harper shuffled to the sink and turned on the water. Her shoulders slumped. Her vision blurred from the buildup of an abundant but not yet fallen rush of tears. A burning in her midsection made her want to double over, slide on the floor and sleep. She stuck her reddened hands under the faucet and tried to wash away the stain of her child's blood. No matter how clear the water ran, she would forever see the red spots on her hands.

The last trace of her living baby girl, who'd brightened her life—made her proud—swirled down the drain with a finality that hit Becky hard. A pounding surge of love rose and crashed down—shattering on the rough rocks on her newly earned, hard-as-granite grief.

Bobbie Jo Stinnett, a soft-spoken, sweet-smiling 23-year-old woman, streaked away from her home in an ambulance. It headed up the road traveled by Chris Law just a short time before. Bobbie Jo was declared dead upon arrival at St. Francis Hospital & Health Services in the nearby county seat of Maryville.

2

The dark blonde drove along a small country road. Up and down the rolling hills. Past empty, harvested fields, over one-lane bridges, past the placid faces of huddled cattle, beyond the cemetery that would soon be home to her victim. Past white farmhouses and faded red barns. Through mile after mile of barren countryside.

Before she reached St. Joseph, Missouri, she took a ramp onto Interstate 29 and headed south. She skirted the town and pushed on to Kansas City. She crossed the Missouri River and entered Kansas. She turned due west on Interstate 70 and made a beeline to Topeka.

She did not travel alone in her dirty red Toyota Corolla. In the seat beside her was a passenger. It slept and cried and slept again. It was not the puppy she claimed she wanted. Beside her was more precious cargo, a newborn infant—my baby, she insisted. My baby. My baby. My baby. The mantra pounded in her head.

What went through her mind as she made the two-and-a-half-hour drive from Skidmore, Missouri, to Topeka, Kansas? Did she believe her own lies that she had given birth to this child? Or did she think that, regardless of how it was born, the infant belonged to her now?

Did she subscribe to the self-serving story she later told her mother—that she found the baby on the floor, whisked it up and ran from the violence committed by some unknown perpetrator? Was she disturbed enough to become convinced of her own falsehoods? Or did she know what she had done?

Is it possible that she beat the plowshares of fantasy into the sword of truth as mile after mile passed beneath her wheels? Or did she instead spend the time plotting and planning her actions to ensure each move was designed to help her get away with murder and retain her stolen prize? Was she self-deluded or was she self-aware?

Whatever she believed, that stark afternoon, at 5:15, she called her husband from the parking lot of Long John Silver's on Southwest Sixth Avenue. She told him that she'd gone to Topeka to do some shopping. Much to her surprise, she said, she went into labor right in the middle of running her errands. She said she'd rushed to the Birth & Women's Center where their beautiful daughter was born.

The man had believed his wife when she told him she was pregnant. He believed her now. He thought he was the father of a newborn baby girl. In his first marriage he'd had three boys. This baby was his first daughter. He was ecstatic. Excitement rippled through his voice as he called to his wife's children from a previous marriage. Only two of the four were at home at the time—a ninth-grader and a senior in high school. He related the good news from their mother. All three of them piled into his pickup and headed north.

The woman sat in her car awaiting her family's arrival at Long John Silver's and picked up her cell phone. She jabbed in the number of the minister at the church where she and her husband were married. Was it a sign of remorse or regret? No, it was merely another step in the perpetuation of the big lie. It was as if the more people shared in her fantasy of the birth of the baby, the more she believed it herself.

She told the preacher about the labor pains that took her by surprise and that as soon as her husband got to Topeka, she and the baby would be heading home. And said she would bring her new daughter by soon.

Grinning from ear to ear, her husband pulled into the parking lot. He and his two passengers clambered out of the truck. He rushed to his wife's side and helped her and the baby settle into the cab of the pickup and then climbed in beside them. Love beamed from his eyes. Love for his daughter. Love for his wife. The two older kids hopped into their mother's car and the high school senior drove, following her father's truck down Highway 75 and State Route 31 to their home in Melvern, Kansas.

This late in December, the sun set by 5 P.M. The mini-caravan drove in darkness down the highway. Traveling south from Topeka, there was no need to pass through the town center of Melvern where Garry's Bar & Grill was the solitary lively venue on Main Street. They approached South Adams Road from the opposite direction.

In the night unlit by streetlights, barren trees stretched eerie branches to the sky in the glare of the headlights. In the pickup truck, the woman clutched the false proof of her fertility to her chest.

At home, the senior used her cell phone to capture images of her mother and the baby she believed was her half-sister. The husband used an RCA camcorder to record the homecoming on videotape and a digital camera preserved the moment in a computer-ready format.

When the initial excitement died down, the woman prepared a makeshift bed for the infant and settled her in for the night. The woman then sat down at her computer and emailed the youngest of her three daughters, who now lived

with a family friend in Alabama because of the irreconcil-
able differences she had with her mother. To the email an-
nouncing the birth, the counterfeit new mother attached a
photo of her new baby, Abigail.

3

A few blocks away from the crime scene in Skidmore, Reverend Harold Hamon, the minister at Skidmore Christian Church, sat at his kitchen table addressing Christmas cards. The day his congregation would join him in the celebration of the birth of Christ was near at hand. Soon voices would rise in jubilation as they sang out the words to "Silent Night," "Hark the Herald Angels Sing" and "Joy to the World." Together they would pay homage to God for his wondrous gift to man—his son, Jesus Christ, the savior.

He had no idea that before the day was over, his thoughts would turn to contemplation of the power of darkness and evil that stalked the world. Had anyone suggested it, he would rebuke their negativity as the next thing to blasphemy. Then his phone rang. A member of his congregation called to report that he'd heard a siren and was concerned. Engrossed in his thoughts and the task at hand, Reverend Hamon had not heard a thing. His parishioner asked, "Was anyone near the church hurt?"

Hamon looked out of his front window and peered across the neighborhood. From his vantage point, he could see the flashing lights just a short distance away. It looked as if the police cars were parked in front of the home of two members of his church, Bobbie Jo and Zeb Stinnett. He was concerned that something went wrong with Bobbie Jo's pregnancy. But there was no way he could have imagined the actual nature of the nightmare that came calling on Elm Street.

Sheriff Espey surveyed the scene in the small bedroom of the Stinnett house. He saw clear signs of a struggle. The bloodstained soles of Bobbie Jo's feet told him that she managed to get to her feet after the attack began. The strands of darkish blond hair clutched in her hands informed him that she did not give up easily. She fought hard with her attacker to jerk those strands out by the roots. The blood clots scattered across the floor indicated that her death was not swift. It had to have passed through at least three distinct phases—the initial assault, Bobbie Jo's collapse and revival, then the fatal attack. The smeared bloody footprints on the floor choreographed a mute testimony to Bobbie Jo's valiant fight for life.

Espey was a proud man—but not too proud to ask for help. The Nodaway County Sheriff's Department was a small outfit. They did not have a team of crime-scene investigators and they did not have sufficient manpower to blanket the countryside. On top of that, in this low-crime county, homicide was a rare event, and their department's experience was limited. Espey placed a call to the Missouri Highway Patrol.

Another priority for the sheriff was Bobbie Jo's husband. As a rule, in his jurisdiction, murder happened one of two ways—either it was a drunken brawl or a domestic violence incident. Was Zeb Stinnett a widowed victim?

Or was he the perpetrator? Before the first hour of the investigation passed, Espey had confirmation that Zeb Stinnett was not responsible for his wife's death. He had never left his job at Kawasaki Motors in Maryville that afternoon. An awareness of his brief moment as a suspect probably didn't cross Zeb's mind that day. His wife was dead. His baby was missing. There was no room for any other concerns.

Soon, people began to talk. The Nodaway County grapevine bore putrid fruit—a truth no one could keep to themselves and yet could hardly speak: Bobbie Jo Stinnett was dead. She was murdered. Her baby could not be found. In Skidmore, speculation fueled rumors and suspicion. They prayed that the killer was not one of their own. They prayed that the newborn baby survived its ordeals. Their voices rose and crowded the pathway to heaven.

Cheryl Huston, Becky Harper's close friend from high school, left her job at Wal-Mart at the end of her shift. On her way out, one of the door greeters stopped her to tell her about the horrible news coming from Skidmore that day. The greeter, however, did not know the victim's name.

As Cheryl drove home, she ran a mental list of all of the pregnant women she knew in town. Only one matched the age of the victim. Only one was eight months pregnant. The only one was her good friend's daughter, Bobbie Jo Stinnett. Her worst fears were confirmed when she drove past Elm Street—official vehicles, flashing lights and yellow crime-scene tape marked the spot.

She never knew a mother and daughter with a closer relationship than the one between Becky and Bobbie Jo. Her heart ached for the burden Becky now carried.

The word spread to the local media and they descended on the crime scene. Espey sealed off the dead-end block to keep them at bay.

An hour and a half into the investigation, the sheriff contacted the state headquarters of the Amber Alert system in Jefferson City. They asked for the hair color, eye color, skin complexion, size and weight of the abduction victim. Espey had no answers. Officials denied his request.

They insisted there was nothing they could do. An Amber Alert had to meet specific criteria. This case did not meet the established standards to issue this public notice—he had no description of the kidnapped child.

Only one person did have that information—the one who abducted Bobbie Jo's baby. With every moment, Espey sensed that person slipping further and further from his grasp.

At the National Center for Missing and Exploited Children outside of Washington, D.C., word of the abduction hit the desk of Cathy Nahirny and she got busy. She pulled information from similar cases. She gathered contact information for the investigators who'd handled the most recent caesarean abduction in Oklahoma one year earlier.

Once she pulled it all together, she turned it over to John Rabun, who forwarded the data on to law enforcement in Missouri. They wanted investigators to know the profile of this kind of offender—to realize that they were not looking for a typical criminal. They wanted the detectives to know they were not alone—an identical crime occurred just two states away twelve months earlier. They wanted them to be able to avail themselves of the knowledge of those law enforcement agencies and not waste time following up on leads that were destined to be unproductive. Cathy and John knew knowledge was power and they wanted the investigators to have all the power they could get to bring this infant home.

The sheriff raced to the hospital and talked to the medical staff, who assured him that the baby was probably still alive. But, they continued, the infant was premature, may have suffered a variety of traumas during the assault—including the possibility of a lack of oxygen—and, thus, had special medical needs. "The newborn will survive if treated. You need to find that baby immediately," they warned.

Espey didn't need to be told that this was the most piv-
otal, time-sensitive moment of his career. He knew he
needed the help of the public. He knew the Amber Alert
would generate thousands of vigilant eyes that would help
track down the kidnapper and the baby. His request might
not meet the criteria, but he was determined to shove his
square peg of information into the neat round hole of the
system. The authorities' stubborn refusal could not—would
not—stand.

He called the home of United States Representative Sam
Graves. The elected official was a quick study. He understood
at once the necessity for cutting through the red tape and
regulations—a child's life was at stake.

It was not just the infant's survival at issue here. Every
passing moment gave the murderous abductor time to travel
further from the scene of the crime—perhaps far enough to
obscure the wrongdoing, hide the baby's identity and separate the infant from its real family for life. Bureaucratic process could not be allowed to aid and abet the kidnapper in
achieving this goal.

Representative Graves had a secret weapon. Not only was
he the congressman for the district, with a certain amount of
power in his own right, he was also the brother of United
States Attorney Todd Graves in Kansas City, Missouri. Sam
had a lot of strings he could pull, and he jerked hard.

Sheriff Espey's call for assistance at the crime scene put
a lot of law enforcement specialists in motion. The first to
head toward Skidmore was Sergeant Dave Merrill of the
Missouri Highway Patrol.

En route, Merrill called Commander Larry Smith at the
St. Joseph's Police Department. St. Joseph was the biggest
city in Missouri north of Kansas City. It had a population of
75,000. It was the town where the Pony Express began and
Jesse James' notorious life came to an end, and on the trail
followed by Lewis and Clark.

Heavy in history but progressive in technology, the police
department's investigative and forensic officers were the best

for miles. Their department's high-tech crime-scene specialists responded to the requests of a number of area counties throughout Northwest Missouri.

After running the out-of-jurisdiction request by Police Chief Mike Hirter, Smith pulled together a team of two investigators and five evidence techs. Then, they put their mobile command post on the road. This twenty-foot-long converted recreational vehicle was equipped with five computerized work stations, an eight-person conference center, a satellite, generator, decontamination shower and a bathroom. It was an invaluable tool at any crime scene. In addition to providing an efficient work space and a secure area for discussion among officers, it was also a retreat where detectives and techs could take a break to refocus and revitalize.

Missouri State Highway Patrol vehicles from around the region congregated in the area around Skidmore. Those officers and Sheriff Espey and his deputies instituted a rigorous search for a small newborn bundle of humanity. They peered in every Dumpster—diving into any whose contents raised the slightest suspicion.

Their eyes scoured roadsides checking out any discarded trash of promising size. At every bridge, they paused to examine the creek beds, streams and riverbanks searching for anything that resembled a baby thrown over the side. At the same time, they kept a keen eye on all the passing traffic, desperate to spot any vehicle approximating the description of the car seen earlier in front of the Stinnett home.

A ticking clock pounded out its beat in every officer's head. Every minute counted. Every passing hour was cause for dread. Desperation fueled their search and their hearts as they searched for a baby they hoped was still alive, but feared was dead. They went door to door canvassing the area in a four-block radius of the Stinnett home.

Investigator Mike Wilson of the detective division was the first member of the St. Joseph Police Department to enter the home at 410 Elm Street. He crossed the front porch and opened the door. Neither the jambs nor the lock displayed any of the telltale signs of forced entry. He stepped into the living room. His eyes scanned over a television, a sofa and an easy chair, looking for anything amiss. Not a single item was out of order. Not one surface was dulled with dust.

In the dining room, the reign of order continued. No signs of any altercation. He spotted a computer next to the wall and made a mental note of its presence.

That room led to the kitchen where the first signs of violence caught his eye. Someone attempted to clean up in the blood-spattered sink. Had the perpetrator paused there and washed his hands? He stored that question in his mind, knowing he needed to find an answer to it before he left the house.

Off to the left of the dining room was a converted bedroom. It was there that the reason for his presence was obvious. The evidence of a struggle was written in red all over the floor.

The victim's body was no longer in place, but the evidence of her life and her fight to maintain it were painted in the blood at his feet. Knowing that the person who died there was a young pregnant woman made his stomach flip.

Wilson sent the crime-scene experts in to recover any type of prints, all stray fibers and every microscopic bit of evidence they could find. Every doorframe, door knob, or table surface, and the counter around the kitchen sink was dusted with black powder. The patterns revealed were lifted in the hope that one would be evidence of a killer who left his mark.

Any place a clothing fiber snagged, tweezers plucked and bagged the thread. Any little thing that betrayed the passage of a human being was gathered, stored and documented.

The blatant and obvious would not be ignored either. The blood on the floor was examined, photographed and analyzed. Samples were taken to determine if all of it was the victim's blood or if the red mass included drops from the attacker or from the infant.

Once Sergeant Wilson finished the orchestration of his team of techs, he turned his attention back to the computer in the kitchen. He placed a call to St. Joseph's forensic computer specialist Curtis Howard. Howard worked on the strike force and in street crimes for three years before moving into computer forensics in 1996. He got additional training every year at the National White Collar Crime Center facility in Fairmont, West Virginia. Now his skills were needed to unravel clues in a far more grisly case.

Wilson asked Howard to come to Skidmore right away and bring his mobile forensics recovery device. The Patriot Act made the investigative process flow far more smoothly. Before that legislation, it would have been necessary to appear before a judge and get a computer-specific search warrant before violating the privacy of the device. Since no one with ownership of the computer—Bobbie Jo or Zeb—were considered suspects, law enforcement could move forward without hesitation or legal complication.

Howard gathered his equipment and headed north—arriving on the scene an hour after receiving the call. He moved the computer from the dining room and out of the crowded house to the relative peace and quiet of the command center parked on the street. He positioned the computer at a work station, plugged it in and booted it up. He knew he would need to image the hard drive—but he also knew the task could take up to six hours. They may not have that much time to locate the infant alive.

That thought struck Howard with a visceral dread. His baby girl Reece was born only a few months earlier this year. Irrational worry about his baby rushed to the front of his mind. He pushed his anxiety away and focused on the job at hand.

He locked down the hard drive and previewed the contents. He doubted he'd find any direct leads, but he had to try. Computer hard drives often yielded unexpected secrets.

At first, it all appeared to be just a normal household PC with ordinary activity. But when he explored chat room use, a clear clue erupted from the idle banter: a mention of a woman, north of Fairfax, Missouri, who was supposed to meet that day with Bobbie Jo.

He typed in a keyword search for "Fairfax." An Internet conversation between happyhavenfarms@hotmail.com, xgringo @hotmail.com and fischer4kids@hotmail.com popped up. The Happy Haven Farms address belonged to Bobbie Jo Stinnett. The Fischer 4 Kids address belonged to a woman self-identified as Darlene Fischer. This woman talked about her four kids, her need to get out of the chat room and into the kitchen to make supper for her children. And she chatted about her plans to drop by the Stinnett house to see Bobbie Jo's puppies the next day—today, December 16, 2004.

The possibility of a dark double meaning to the Fischer 4 Kids address did not cross Detective Howard's thoughts. All he envisioned was a woman who'd planned to come to Bobbie Jo's home on the same day that she was murdered. A woman who may have seen something relevant during her visit—she may have observed the perpetrator without knowing it. He knew they needed to talk to that woman immediately.

Espey, Merrill and every available highway patrol officer in the vicinity headed to Fairfax in neighboring Atchison County. No matter how hard they searched, they could find no record of Darlene Fischer in the area—no phone number, no address, no indication that she'd ever lived anywhere near the town. Still they persevered—looking, questioning, prodding the community's memory. The name did not sound familiar to anyone they encountered—not to law enforcement or the public at large. They had to find this woman. And they had to find her now. They radiated out from the town center probing memories along the way.

Around midnight, they thought they caught a break. Highway patrol encountered a car going at high speed in Atchison County just twenty-two miles from Skidmore. It matched the description of the vehicle seen in front of the Stinnett house early that afternoon. Sheriff Espey abandoned his futile search for Darlene Fischer and joined in the pursuit. As they streaked through the night at dangerous speeds, they feared their target would lose control of the fleeing car, causing it to wreck. Bobbie Jo's baby could be in that car—and the infant could still be alive. If they could effect a stop without harming anyone inside, they might be able to rescue the child tonight.

It was more than a professional objective for Espey. Just six days before, his daughter Jennifer gave birth to his grandson, Benjamin Wyatt. It took little use of his imaginative powers to conjure up a parallel between Bobbie Jo and Jennifer in his mind—to imagine little Benjamin Wyatt as the missing child. He visualized the possibility that it could have been his daughter in a pool of blood—it could have been his grandson fleeing with a madman through the darkness of the night. He fought the rising edge of desperation as he pursued the speeding car he had in his sights.

When, at last, law enforcement succeeded in halting the racing driver, Espey's high hopes plummeted. There was no baby—just a reckless driver who made a bad judgment call. In disgust and discouragement, they showered him with tickets and went back to their frantic search.

At 12:30 A.M., on December 17, the Amber Alert—at last—streaked from coast to coast. The work of Congressman Graves hurdled the last bureaucratic barrier. The statement asked people to look out for and report any abandoned or discarded bloody clothing or towels. It warned that the infant could have health issues and would have a freshly cut umbilical cord.

The release of this information nationwide eased Espey's anxiety a bit. He doubted that the kidnapper and the baby were inside the boundaries of the state of Missouri any longer. Now, he would have eyes searching everywhere.

The Amber Alert brought more than an army of observers to the cause. It also was a clarion call to media across the nation. This story was as hot as they get. Broadcast and cable networks scrambled to get reporters and camera operators on the scene. As they booked flights and made arrangements to head to Missouri, many of them wondered: Skidmore? Where have I heard that name before? One by one, their memories resurrected the old news from the small Missouri town.

More than twenty-three years ago, the nation recoiled from the horror emanating from the northwest corner of the state. Another person died in the middle of the day in Skidmore. Although there were thirty-five witnesses to *that* crime, the case remained unsolved.

4

Ken McElroy was a bully, a stalker, a drive-by shooter, a livestock rustler, a wife-beater and a pedophile. He dominated the town of Skidmore like a gangster. To know him was to fear him. But it was not the way Ken McElroy lived that put Skidmore on the map. It was the way he died.

He was born in 1934, the fifteenth of sixteen children. He grew up in the Skidmore area, where he dropped out of school without mastering the ability to read or write.

As a teenager, McElroy spent many nights tramping through the woods with his buddies and his hunting dogs searching for hapless raccoons. His passion for coon-hunting worked well for a man who felt most comfortable lurking in the dark of the night. It was an inclination that served him well in his other nocturnal occupation—stealing from his neighbors.

He wasn't particular about what he stole—from gasoline to antiques—if he could fence it, he took it. Livestock theft, though, was his specialty. There was no branding requirement in the state of Missouri, making it easy for McElroy to bribe auction houses to sell his ill-gotten goods. After his successful plunders, he often taunted his victims by flashing wads of money he'd obtained at their expense. He loved to visit the D&G tavern and laugh in their faces as they cried in their beer.

McElroy was just 18 when he married his first teenage bride, Oleta. The couple moved to Denver for a short time. McElroy found no financial success in Colorado—not in legitimate work or in criminal activity. They moved back to northwest Missouri.

McElroy strayed from the marital bed early and often. He liked to spend time on junior high school grounds assessing the "young meat" at play. He wooed and bedded many young girls from poor, uneducated families. If one of his victims got pregnant, he used a combination of payoffs and threats to discourage the girls' parents from pressing criminal charges.

After a few years, when Oleta was no longer the sweet young thing he wed, he tossed her out of his home, divorced her and went on the hunt for another wife.

Using his rough, hillbilly good looks and cheap tokens of affection, he snared 15-year-old Sharon. His fidelity to his marriage vows did not last long. As soon as Sharon was pregnant, he wooed 13-year-old Sally. The young girl at first refused his sexual advances, but when McElroy threatened to kill her father, Sally acquiesced and moved in with Ken and Sharon.

By 1964, McElroy was the father of seven children, courtesy of Sharon and Sally. With both women caring for newborns, and Sharon pregnant again, McElroy's eye roamed to another teenager, 15-year-old Alice Wood from St. Joseph, Missouri.

*   *   *

After years of getting away with his outrageous thieving behavior, McElroy faced his first livestock rustling charge in
1972. His Kansas City lawyer Richard McFadin got the case
dismissed. It was the first time McElroy teamed up with Mc-
Fadin. But it would not be the last.

5

McElroy abandoned Sharon, Sally and his houseful of children in the early 70s. He moved into another home with his newest conquest, Alice. Soon he encountered another naïve girl, Marcia. In no time, he once again had two females in his household sharing his bed. But two girls were not enough to slake his lust. He still had the energy and desire to pursue a blonde eighth-grader named Trena.

After a childhood in poverty, 12-year-old Trena McCloud was easy to impress with cheap trinkets and rides in McElroy's new pickup truck. To counter the spread of his aging paunch, he tried to recapture his youth and gain access to this new adolescent heart by dyeing his hair a deep Elvis black.

He hired a boy her age to pick her up at her home and walk her over to a designated meeting place. When McElroy was through with Trena for the day, the boy escorted her home. McElroy designed these convoluted arrangements to keep Trena's parents unaware of his seduction of their daughter. Whispered rumors of the relationship spread through Skidmore, but no one dared anger McElroy by telling the girl's parents. The truth, however, could not remain a public secret for long. In ninth grade, Trena became pregnant and dropped out of school. She left her parents' home and moved in with McElroy. Upon her arrival, he shoved Marcia out of the household.

Even with one rival gone, neither Alice nor Trena were pleased with the arrangement—both wanted to be the only woman in Ken's bed. They bickered day in and day out. Despite the beatings administered by McElroy to bring them in line and return peace to the home, the girls simply could not get along.

Alice had enough. She wanted out. Sixteen days after Trena gave birth to her son, Alice made her move. She took refuge in the one place she knew she'd find sympathy—the home of Trena's mother and stepfather. Although McElroy discarded lovers like burnt-out disposable lighters, he could not tolerate it when one walked out on him. He tracked Alice down and brought her back to his house at gunpoint.

McElroy beat Alice with a brutality that was extreme even by his vicious standards. Then, he turned his gun on Trena and ordered her to strip naked. While Alice watched, he then engaged in sex acts with Trena designed to humiliate her and terrify Alice.

When he finished punishing the girls, he forced Trena out of the house and into his pickup. They drove to Trena's mother's house. Fourteen-year-old Trena trembled in fear as she sat in the cab of the truck watching McElroy go inside with a gas can and a rifle. She feared hearing her mother's scream. Or her stepfather's shout. But all she heard was a rifle blast. Followed by a brief yip. No one was home but the family dog. McElroy shot him dead. He sloshed gasoline throughout the house and in a trail running out the door. Safely outside, he tossed a match toward the entryway. Trena watched in horror as the flame blossomed and raced inside.

McElroy slammed the truck into gear and zoomed away from the scene. Out the rear window, Trena saw the flames lick the sky before her mother's home faded from view. The house burned to the ground—the structure and its contents a total loss.

Two days later, Trena traveled to Mound City to take her son to the doctor there. Her darting eyes and shaky voice told the physician that all was not well in this young woman's life.

At his prodding, the words tumbled out of Trena's mouth. Between sobs, she told the story of the arson, abuse and intimidation that led to the destruction of her parents' home. The doctor contacted authorities. Trena's son was placed in foster care and the doctor admitted her to the hospital where she was heavily tranquilized—in part because she was emotionally distraught and in part to keep her safe from her tormentor. After her release from the hospital, Trena found safe haven at the home of her son's foster parents. There Trena answered the questions posed to her by law enforcement. In June 1973, they arrested McElroy on charges of arson, assault and rape. He was released on a $2,500 bond.

McElroy made a beeline to the Kansas City office of his attorney and plunked $15,000 cash on his desk—$5,000 for each felony count. McFadin informed his client that with Trena's testimony, these charges might be impossible to beat.

The Maryville safe house location of the two refugees from McElroy's wrath was supposed to be a well-protected secret. Nevertheless, McElroy soon hunted them down and began a campaign of harassment and threats.

He parked outside the home for hours staring at the windows. He called at all times of the day and night, threatening everyone in the home. In one call, he promised to kidnap the family's daughter from her school so that he could make a trade with them for Trena. He committed no overt act of violence, though. In this time before stalking laws, all law enforcement could do was talk to him and try to persuade him to leave the people in that house alone. They were impotent to stop him. And McElroy was not one to listen to reason or to be intimidated by an officer of the law.

Trena's nerves were rubbed raw, and her level of fear elevated with each passing day. Ultimately, the pressure McElroy applied broke the young girl's resolve. She relented to his demands and moved in with him once again.

McElroy knew he was almost home free. Trena was back under his control. His unflappable lawyer, high-profile Kansas City attorney Richard McFadin, was geared up to beat the arson and domestic violence charges. One more maneuver would make it a sure thing. McElroy's third wife, Sharon, was all that stood in his way.

On cue, Sharon paid a visit to McFadin to request a divorce from McElroy. The second the divorce was final, McElroy obtained the signature of Trena's mother on an affidavit authorizing marriage. McElroy and 15-year-old Trena were married that same day before a judge with attorney McFadin as their witness.

After the service that mocked the sanctity of marriage, the defense lawyer called the prosecutor and informed him with glee that the wedding was a fait accompli. Trena—now McElroy's wife—could no longer be compelled to testify against his client. Trena was the linchpin of the prosecution case. They had other evidence against McElroy, but without Trena's cooperation, success in the courtroom seemed impossible. The charges were dropped. It was just one more set of criminal charges that McFadin brushed away for his felonious client.

A couple of years later, Skidmore resident Romaine Henry was outside working in a shed on his 1,000-acre farm when he heard gunshots ring out nearby. He hopped into his pickup and followed the sound. On a gravel road that bordered his property, Romaine encountered McElroy standing by his own truck with a shotgun in his hands.

McElroy pointed the barrel inside Romaine's vehicle and asked, "Were you the dirty son of a bitch over at my place in a white Pontiac?"

"I don't know what you're talking about, McElroy."

McElroy pulled the trigger, shooting Romaine in the side. As the terrified farmer dove out of his truck to seek shelter, McElroy pulled the trigger again, lodging buckshot into Romaine's forehead and right cheek. After that shot, McElroy's shotgun jammed and he made a hasty retreat.

Following a trip to the hospital in Maryville, Romaine pressed charges. Authorities arrested McElroy the next day. Facing charges of assault with intent to kill, McElroy denied being at the scene of the crime, got bailed out of jail and headed straight to McFadin. His lawyer got a change of venue and McElroy faced a jury unfamiliar with any of his past escapades.

In his defense, two of his coon-hunting friends took the stand and swore that McElroy was nowhere near Romaine's farm during the time the shooting occurred. The jury found those men more credible than the victim and others who testified that they saw McElroy speeding away from the scene.

The jury acquitted McElroy, and the folks of Skidmore went into shock. McElroy rubbed it in deep—telling anyone who would listen that he could have killed Romaine Henry and gotten away with that, too.

6

It looked like, with McFadin's help, things would always go McElroy's way. In July 1981, though, after McFadin helped McElroy walk away from twenty-two felony charges unscathed, prosecutor David Baird actually got a conviction in the shooting of 70-year-old Bo Bowenkamp.

The argument that resulted in Bo's shooting started over a piece of candy. A few of McElroy's children stopped in Bo's B&B grocery store. The kids made their candy selections and jostled each other at the register. One of the littlest girls walked out of the shop without paying for the piece of candy in her hand. When the clerk shouted out to the child, the oldest McElroy girl grabbed the candy from the little one's hand and tossed it on the rack. Robbed of her candy without understanding why, the child burst into tears.

Bo and Lois Bowenkamp figured it was all a big misunderstanding and attempted to patch things up. Their efforts were in vain. It all ended in a stalemate—the McElroy children swore never to shop there again, and the Bowencamps banned all McElroys from their store.

Ken McElroy and Trena showed up twenty minutes later, bellowing, cursing and issuing threats. After this badgering, Bo refused to sell McElroy the pack of smokes he wanted to buy.

That night, McElroy's truck drove past the Bowencamp home again and again. A deputy sheriff told the elderly couple not to worry. McElroy "won't do nothin'," he said.

McElroy showed up at their home and knocked on the door. "Lois, I'll give you one hundred bucks if you challenge Trena to a street fight and then we can call it all quits."

"That's absurd," Lois said.

The next morning, Ken and Trena were outside the Bowencamps' door taunting Lois to come out and fight. Lois called the cops. On his police scanner in his truck, McElroy heard the dispatcher sending officers his way. He was long gone before the state highway patrolman and a deputy sheriff pulled up at the Bowencamps' home.

Once again, the law was on McElroy's side. As long as he committed no overt act, law enforcement was powerless to stop his harassment. Even when the Bowencamps reported that McElroy was shooting off his shotgun in front of their house, no report was filed.

The shop was closed for the day on July 8 while Bo met with an air-conditioner repairman. He was out back cutting up cardboard boxes when McElroy pulled up and commenced harassing Bo again. Bo tried to ignore him, but that only enraged McElroy. He pulled a shotgun out of his truck, pulled the trigger and dropped Bo where he stood.

McElroy was arrested that night. He claimed innocence and the next morning was released on a $30,000 bond. That night, Ken and Trena sat in the D&G Tavern sipping beer and daring anyone to mention Bo.

Bo, meanwhile, spent ten days in the hospital recovering from the gunshot wound to his neck. For a full year after that, he was unable to speak above a whisper. It was more than a year before the last of the shotgun pellets rose to the surface of his neck like a boil. Doctors lanced the ugly red protrusion and removed the pieces of metal.

Bo's daughter, Cheryl Huston, still worked at the family store, but no longer lived at home. She had a family of her own now, but she was frightened by the incident and scared of Ken McElroy. "I woke up terrified. I spent all day terrified. I went to bed terrified."

She carried a shotgun with her everywhere she went. One day, she forgot to carry it out of the house and to the truck. When she climbed in, her 2-year-old daughter said, "Mommy, where's your gun?"

With that simple question, Cheryl realized embracing her fear was no way to live—and no way to raise her children. She never carried her shotgun with her again. Still, she took precautions. While most mothers posted their children's birthday party announcement in the paper, Cheryl did not. She did not want to alert Ken McElroy, who knew her children were the grandchildren of Bo Bowenkamp.

Although Bo was old and bedridden, McElroy continued his campaign of harassment. He threatened the Bowenkamps, the minister who visited Bo in the hospital and anyone who expressed any sympathy for their fate. He even pulled a shotgun on the part-time town marshal who was planning to testify for the prosecution, telling him he would kill anyone who put him behind bars. The marshal reported this incident, but when the county authorities did not back him up and revoke McElroy's bail, the marshal turned in his badge to the mayor.

McElroy's shooting of Bo was a pretty open-and-shut case. However, since McFadin's legal maneuverings earned a change of venue, neither the judge nor the jury who heard the case was aware of McElroy's past. The jury gave him a short 2-year sentence. The judge released McElroy on bond for twenty-five days while his attorney filed an appeal. He was due back in court on July 10.

A few days later, McElroy took center stage in Skidmore's

D&G Tavern. He flaunted an assault rifle with a bayonet as
he demonstrated how he'd finish off the job on Bowencamp.
He bragged he'd put a bullet in Bowencamp's head and then
carve him up with the blade. Prosecutor Baird tried to get
McElroy's bail revoked after this incident, but the judge
thought July 10 was soon enough to put McElroy back behind bars.

The townfolk awoke to the day of McElroy's hearing with
plans to travel to court to encourage his immediate incarceration. Then they got the word that the legal proceedings were
postponed until July 20 because McElroy's attorney had a
scheduling conflict.

About sixty distraught citizens gathered in the American
Legion hall to meet with Nodaway County Sheriff Danny
Estes. They discussed forming a neighborhood watch, but the
suggestion generated little enthusiasm. They wanted a more
proactive approach.

While Estes drove away from the meeting with the frustrated Skidmore citizens and headed back to his office in
Maryville, trouble was brewing. McElroy got word of the
town gathering. He drove to Main Street and parked his new
Chevrolet Silverado pickup truck in plain sight. He sauntered into the D&G Tavern to gloat to his neighbors.

The disgruntled crowd of men heard the word that McElroy was at the D&G. They all moved down the street and
gathered outside. About thirty men in the crowd went inside.
Some ordered a soda or a beer—others just stood and stared
at the man who tormented their days.

McElroy ordered a six-pack to go. He sauntered out of
the bar with his wife Trena by his side. Most of the men
who'd been inside the bar followed them out and joined the
others still waiting outside on Main Street at Newton's corner. As they watched, Trena climbed into the passenger seat.
McElroy hefted his weight up behind the wheel.

McElroy smiled—pleased with the fear, anxiety and
anger he saw on the faces of his neighbors. He basked in the
glow of their hatred. He didn't want to back up and drive off

right away, he was enjoying the drama too much not to perpetuate it a bit longer.

He put a Camel to his lips. He pulled out a lighter. Held it
up with a flourish. His thumb flicked the striking wheel. The
flame flared. The first shot rang out. Two shots came from
the left. Four exploded in the rear.

Men hit the ground. Others fled the scene. Eyes met then
slid away. A blood-spattered Trena leaped out of the truck
screaming: One man in the crowd grabbed her and rushed
her out of the line of fire. Then silence hit the streets of Skidmore. And an unspoken oath was sworn. Eyes met and held.
Heads nodded.

Estes—still en route to Maryville—got a call over his radio. He raced back to Skidmore. When he arrived, the crowd
had dispersed, weapons were concealed and McElroy was
dead.

Despite the presence of dozens of witnesses, no one saw
anything. The only people who called in on the tip hotline
were media. Despite the work of a task force of twenty-three
officers from six law enforcement agencies, and testimony
from Trena and others present at the shooting, the grand jury
adjourned without issuing an indictment against anyone.
They ruled that McElroy "died from bullets fired by a person
or persons unknown."

The vigilante incident drew media attention from across
the globe. Editorials by newspapers at home and abroad expressed outrage at the community's act of violence and their
willingness to remain silent. The citizens of Skidmore, however, were sanguine about the event. As Postmaster Jim
Hartman told reporters, the killers should get a medal. He
compared them to the inventors of penicillin—"Nobody
tried to hang them for finding a way to kill a germ."

The only regret any of the townspeople expressed was
about the damage to McElroy's shiny new Silverado.

Now, decades later, one of their own was an *innocent* victim. She lived just three blocks away from the place where

McElroy died. And Skidmore—still shaking from the tre-mors of a bully's death more than twenty years ago—was outraged, terrified and determined to secure justice in the death of Bobbie Jo.

7

Out in the mobile command center post on Elm Street in Skidmore, Detective Curtis Howard finished his preliminary review of the Stinnetts' computer without finding any additional information to aid in the search for Darlene Fischer. He needed an IP address before he could uncover more. That task was difficult if not impossible to accomplish in the middle of the night.

Around 2 A.M., he packed up the computer and his equipment and took it all to his office at St. Joseph's Police Department. He no longer had the time to do the imaging. In just a few hours, he had a training session scheduled. The computer work could not wait. Someone had to pick up where he left off and move the forensics examination of the PC forward. He called on the highway patrol's computer wizard Corporal Jeff Owens.

When Owens arrived in St. Joseph, Howard briefed him on what steps he had taken and the questions his preliminary search raised. Owens transported the computer an hour down the road to his base of operations, the multi-agency Heart of America Regional Computer Forensic Laboratory in Kansas City, Missouri.

This facility—designed to coordinate and enhance the forensic computer capabilities of law enforcement in the region—was based on a model developed in San Diego. That model was first copied by the Dallas field office of the FBI in 2000. Eight agencies in north Texas participated and benefited from that center.

After passing the Patriot Act of 2001, Congress took a look at those two offices and charged the FBI with opening more facilities across the country. In 2003 two more labs were in operation—the one where Owens worked and another in Chicago, Illinois.

Corporal Owens linked Bobbie Jo's computer to his own. His computer was equipped with a program that would not permit the erasure of any of the data. It also had software that enabled real-time viewing of all the data in the computer he examined.

At 5 A.M., Sheriff Espey abandoned his search in Fairfax and headed back to Nodaway County. He was convinced that Darlene Fischer existed only on the Internet. It was up to the computer forensics specialists to solve the mystery of her true identity.

Espey was grateful for the news coverage reporters provided on the Amber Alert for Bobbie Jo's baby. He did not want the media getting in the way at the crime scene on Elm Street. But he did want them as an ally.

He knew the local press was ravenous for any information and that the gathering storm cloud of national media would be unstoppable. With a murder this fresh and a child still missing, it was hard to distinguish what information needed to be withheld to solve the crime and what needed to be released to find the baby.

By the time Espey got back to Nodaway County, media

crawled all over Skidmore like ants on a sugar pile—and more were arriving with every passing hour. He set up an area next to the jail for the reporters and cameramen, and promised regular press conferences. The journalists took the bait and headed out of Skidmore to the county seat of Maryville.

It was all a surreal experience for Espey. A little more than a year earlier, Espey was battered and reeling after election night. He very nearly watched his career dissolve before his eyes. Nearly ten thousand votes were cast in the November 2 election of 2004. Espey won by a mere fourteen votes. Now he stood in the national spotlight clutching the desperate hope that everything he did would validate the faith of the voters who reelected him to office.

As truth and rumor swirled through the area, it was easy pickings for the media. Everybody knew everybody—and everyone had something to say. The desire to help find the baby overcame the natural reticence in Skidmore to speak about one of their own to anyone from outside of the community.

As reporters picked up each fresh scent, they lobbed ceaseless questions at Sheriff Ben Espey every time he stepped outside. Initially, he told them, "We're going to work this case as a homicide right now. We're not going to tell you that it is. We're not going to tell you that it isn't."

A lead regarding two men, a woman and a black-market baby-selling ring led Espey to announce that they were looking for these three persons of interest. At the same time, he informed the media that they wanted to locate a 1980s or 1990s red two-door hatchback—possibly a Honda.

Whoever committed this act knew what to do, he told them, and "most likely had some medical knowledge." He said that everything they now knew indicated that "Somebody was wanting a baby awful bad."

Law enforcement had checked up on every documented deviant in the county by the time Espey called a major news conference late Friday morning. Now that the authorities

explored a more promising lead, the sheriff was more forthcoming.

He stepped to the microphone in a fresh, smooth khaki
uniform that belied his sleepless night on the job. Atop his
head sat a Nodaway County Sheriff's Department baseball
cap. The brim shaded the exhaustion and anxiety in his eyes.
His tall, square-shouldered, stoic image spoke of a man a
whole county could trust. He appeared in control of himself,
in control of the situation and even in control of fate itself.
That image concealed an internal swamp of rising desperation and doubt.

He explained that an autopsy was now under way in Jack-
son County. "More than likely, our victim was strangled and
probably deceased when the baby was removed from her
womb. The mother was eight months pregnant, so we're
looking at a one-month-premature baby that was removed
with the umbilical cord cut.

"And for now it looks like to us that the evidence shows
that the baby was probably wrapped up and taken out of the
home. That puts us to looking for a red car that had been sitting in the driveway from two-thirty to three, which we're
going to rule was the time when all this took place."

In response to their questions, he told them that neither
the investigators nor the family knew of any suspects. "This
was a nice lady—everybody said this was a nice lady. She
didn't have any enemies. They just couldn't understand how
anyone could do this."

A reporter asked, "Is this baby-selling—is that still a
theory?"

"That is still a theory."

The reporter continued. "This is something I've never
heard of—black-market sale of children. I mean, you've
been doing this a long time . . ."

"I've never heard of it," Espey said. He added that one
child abduction specialist never heard of one working in
the United States, either, but the FBI now had six agents
searching on the Internet and calling states to find out if

one had developed in recent months. "That lead," he added, "is possibly going up in smoke. The third party has misled us."

And, as in every other crime whose inexplicable horror stirs up primitive fears, a reporter raised the question of a satanic ritual. "Not here," Espey insisted. "I've been in law enforcement here for twenty years and we have not dealt with any cults in Nodaway County."

"Sir, where does the investigation go from here?" another reporter shouted out.

Espey sighed. He opened and shut his mouth, struggling to find the right answer.

"Forward," an unidentified voice rang out.

Espey grinned in appreciation. "Forward," he said. The crowd chuckled in response. "It follows whatever leads we get."

It seemed to Espey that every time investigators got a new lead, the press was just a step or two behind them. He hoped his cooperation and openness would ensure that they worked with law enforcement, not against them.

Half a continent away, in Franklin, North Carolina, rat terrier breeder Dyanne Siktar sat down at her computer. As usual, her first stop was Annie's Rat Terrier Rest Area. Her attention riveted on an unusual post. "Don't know if anyone knows this rat terrier breeder but Bobbie Jo Stinnett was murdered."

Dyanne jumped from that website to CNN.com and read the full story. A connection clicked in her mind. She bounced back to the rat terrier boards. She found what she sought—a December 15 exchange between Darlene Fischer and Bobbie Jo Stinnett.

It began with a post from Darlene to Bobbie Jo:

> I was recommended to you by Jason Dawson and have been unable to reach you by either phone or email. Please get in touch with me soon as we are considering the purchase of one of your puppies . . .

Bobbie Jo responded right away and the two spent twenty minutes in back-and-forth instant messaging. Bobbie Jo wrapped up their Internet conversation:

> Darlene,
> I've emailed you with the directions so we can meet. I do so hope that the email reaches you. Great chatting with you on messenger. And do look forward to chatting with you tomorrow a.m.
>   Thanks Jason, and talk to you soon Darlene!
>   Have a great evening
>   Bobbie

Dyanne picked up the phone and called information for the number of the FBI in Missouri. She was connected to Special Agent Kurt Lipanovich. She gave him the URL for the rat terrier board and, most important, the IP address of the message sent by Darlene Fischer to Bobbie Jo.

Lipanovich's phone rang again as soon as he hung up with Dyanne. It was Jeff Owens, who had just uncovered an IP address—the same one Lipanovich just received.

The agent contacted Senior Security Specialist Melissa Erwin at Qwest Communications, who confirmed that her company hosted that address. Performing a reverse domain name system search, she pinpointed a Topeka, Kansas, server. Now the investigators had a limited geographic area for their search. They hit the road and gathered their forces in Kansas.

Erwin continued her digging. She determined that the user accessed a server through a dial-up connection. The telephone number making that call late on the afternoon of December 15 originated from 32419 South Adams Road in Melvern, Kansas.

The investigators centered in Topeka raced thirty miles southwest to Melvern, a tiny town with a population of 400—just barely bigger than Skidmore. Six FBI agents and Kansas law enforcement officials gathered around the rural farmhouse of Kevin and Lisa Montgomery. When they arrived, no one was at home. Combining Chris Law's description of the car he'd seen at the Stinnett home with information from the Kansas vehicle registration database, they would know the Montgomerys were on their way home the second they spotted a dirty red Toyota Corolla.

The FBI was willing to assume responsibility for the case now—in fact, they insisted on it. The investigation had moved out of the jurisdiction of both the Missouri Highway Patrol and the Nodaway County Sheriff's Office. This power play raised the age-old specter of conflict between federal and local authorities. To Sheriff Espey, this was his case. The victims were his responsibility. He was not dropping the reins and walking away.

Espey sent the most effective interrogator he knew to the scene—Detective Randy Strong of Maryville Public Safety. Espey's orders were clear: "You don't stop for anybody. You just go in the house and don't let anyone get in your way."

With Detective Don Fritz riding shotgun, Strong raced at 125 miles per hour from Maryville to Melvern. He made the trip in a record one hour and twenty minutes. Throughout the drive, he kept his cell phone line open in constant communication with Espey. He maintained that connection as they waited with other law enforcement officials for the arrival of the residents of the farmhouse.

8

The morning of December 17, Kevin and Lisa bundled up the baby, hopped in the car and headed up South Adams Road. Red-tailed hawks soared overhead or perched with seeming disinterest on fence posts—their large white chests glistening in the sun of a new day.

Most of the trees alongside the road were dormant and bare. The monotony was broken by the occasional evergreen and the odd dusty gold orbs hanging from the branches and lying at the feet of the black walnut trees.

A frugal farm wife like Lisa Montgomery would see bounty in that wild crop. Lovers of the black walnut gathered up the fruit this time of year and spread them across their basement floors to dry. When the outer shells darkened and turned brittle, they'd carry them out to the driveway and run them over a few times to dislodge the inner shell from its covering. Anyone who attempted to remove the outer surface by hand would have fingers marked for weeks with a deep brown stain that no amount of Lava soap scrubbing could wear away.

The uncovered shells would not yield to a nutcracker. It took a hammer to shatter that surrounding casing and retrieve the nutmeat. After all that work, the occasional dud walnut—its contents shriveled and inedible—was a major disappointment. Many would wonder why anyone would bother going to all that trouble. But those who did knew the rewards—the satisfaction of living off the earth coupled with the pleasure of eating a walnut with ten times the flavor of a store-bought English walnut. That joy in harvesting bounty from the land was a bedrock value of agricultural communities across the Midwest.

About 9:30, Kevin, Lisa and the baby they named Abigail made it to the Whistle Stop Cafe for breakfast. The Whistle Stop was in the middle of the block-long strip of buildings that was downtown Melvern.

As they stepped through the door, the mouthwatering aroma of sausage and bacon sizzling on the grill and biscuits baking in the oven made their stomachs growl in anticipation. Inside, the café was small, cozy and down home. Up the middle, two long groups of wood-grained Formica tables butted end to end from the front door to the kitchen. On either side, individual tables for four ran up the length of the side walls. All the tables were flanked by rigid chairs of black metal with maroon vinyl seats and backs.

The two side walls were decorated with old photographs, baskets and an assortment of antique kitchen tools with their red and green handles and splotchy rust spots. In celebration of Christmas, a tree covered with white lights stood in one corner and a clear glass bud vase filled with artificial red poinsettias adorned each table.

The menus featured good, old-fashioned diner fare with daily home-cooked specials—chili and meatloaf were sell-out favorites in the cold weather months. The pies were homemade and the coffee was just fifty cents a cup.

Country music played at a low level—too soft to cover

the occasional clank and scrape from the cooking area in the back. A tall counter with a cash register blocked a complete view of the kitchen, but it was still partially visible to most of the diners.

Kevin and Lisa rarely patronized the café, but Kevin's parents were well known among the regulars. The couple sat down at a small single table and Lisa set the baby carrier on the floor by her feet. They ordered fried eggs, bacon and hash browns.

As in most small establishments, the arrival of a baby—any baby—was an event that generated happy excitement. Everyone wanted to see her. All made cooing sounds in the infant's direction with the hope that they would be rewarded by a gassy imitation of a smile. One of the customers carried the baby from table to table showing the little treasure to the dozen or so people present while Kevin and Lisa ate. Kevin's eyes sparkled. His grin was so big and so constant that it was a challenge for him to chew his meal.

Whistle Stop owner Kathy Sage scowled with irritation. "Lisa, you don't bring a newborn out in public," she scolded.

"Yeah, it's only a day old," Lisa said.

"We didn't know you were pregnant."

"Most people didn't," Lisa said and turned her attention back to her breakfast.

Despite her sharp words to Lisa, Kathy couldn't help admiring the baby. She smiled down at the pretty, petite infant in her pink bonnet. The Amber Alert Kathy heard on the news that morning did not cross her mind.

Kevin's boss, Darrell Schultze, was there too. He hadn't turned on the television or radio yet that day and was unaware that authorities issued an alert. Nonetheless, the presence of the baby gave him cause for alarm. The baby herself was one of the cutest Darrell had ever seen, but the timing of her arrival made him uncomfortable. "Where in the world did you get this baby?" he asked the couple.

After Lisa explained the story of the baby's birth the day

before in Topeka, Darrell said, "You didn't look that close to delivery when I saw you a week ago."

Kevin said the baby was small—Darrell could see that—then added that Lisa never shown much during any of her pregnancies.

Darrell asked Kevin about the birth experience and Kevin told him that he hadn't been there. "I didn't know about the baby till I got home and Lisa called me from Topeka."

"You should have been there, Kevin. You can get off from work for that. Why didn't you call him, Lisa?"

"I tried," Lisa said, "but I couldn't get hold of him."

Something was not right with that answer. Acme Sign was Darrell's company. He knew that it was always possible to get a message to any of his employees during the day—even for much more minor things than the birth of a baby. But he just complimented them on the baby and said nothing more.

After eating, the couple went up the street two blocks and around the corner to the parsonage of the First Church of God, where Kevin, Lisa and Kevin's parents regularly worshiped. They wanted Reverend Mike Wheatley and his wife to see the baby.

When the Wheatleys opened the door, Kevin's grin was so big it obliterated his cheeks. Lisa looked very tired—just like someone who'd given birth the day before. She was more quiet than usual, but the Wheatleys didn't read much into that. They just blamed her tight lips on exhaustion.

They were a bit taken aback, though, by the trio on their doorstep because for months they had not believed that Lisa was really pregnant. They suspected that she only claimed to be to get attention. But there before their eyes was proof of the reality of her pregnancy. Nonetheless, they thought it odd that the Montgomerys were bringing the baby around to visit so soon.

Despite the surprising nature of the visit, the minister and his wife took turns holding the baby for about an hour. Lisa told them that she and Kevin selected "Abigail" because they wanted a biblical name for their child. Abigail was an obscure but real reference to one of King David's wives in the Old Testament. The Wheatleys noticed a little scratch on the baby's cheek as if she had gouged herself with her tiny fingernail. They observed a small bruise on the back of her hand. Neither of those little injuries seemed out of place, but they could not understand why the infant's head was not misshapen from passing through the birth canal just the day before.

Kevin and Lisa then drove down to Lyndon, Kansas—the seat of Osage County. They stopped by the Lyndon County Courthouse, a large, blocky, tan structure built in 1921 in the center of town. They entered the high-ceilinged halls of the first floor with its shoulder-height pinkish marble panels on the walls. When it was new the courthouse must have been the ultimate in elegant formality. Now it was dated and tired. It was a clean and presentable building, but no amount of scrubbing could wash away the vague musty smell, and decades of use robbed even the purest surfaces of their sparkle.

Kevin, Lisa and baby ascended the long flight of marble steps to the second floor. Their first stop was the county appraiser's office, where Lisa's weekend coworker at Casey's General Store worked on weekdays. Lisa's friend was not there—all the staff of that office was out for a celebratory Christmas meal together. The only person behind the counter was an employee of the County Clerk's office minding the desk in their absence.

Kevin, Lisa and baby Abigail went down one door to the county clerk's office. The couple beamed as that staff oohed and aahed over the infant. Lisa shared her tale of the baby's birth—the surprise when her water burst and the experience of driving with labor pains to the birthing center.

Their next stop was the home of Lisa's ex-husband, Carl Boman, and his new wife, Vanessa. The couple rented a house in Lyndon from Lisa's mother, Judy.

With defiance on her face, Lisa showed the baby to her

former spouse—the father of her four children. Carl did not know what to say.

Vanessa pulled Kevin aside and asked, "Is this really your baby?"

"Yes," Kevin said, his forehead creasing in befuddlement at her question.

"Are you sure Lisa didn't buy it somewhere or steal it from someone?"

Kevin looked at Vanessa as if she'd lost her mind. He told Lisa it was time to leave. Lisa and Kevin then headed up State Route 31 back to their home in Melvern.

Although Lisa's mother, Judy, lived on a farm in the outskirts of Lyndon, they did not take the baby for a visit. Unaware of the addition to her daughter's household the day before and unaware of the Amber Alert that filled the airwaves, Judy was surprised by the phone call from one of her friends who worked at the courthouse. The woman congratulated her on being a grandmother again.

Knowing her daughter's history, Judy said, "Yeah, right. She either stole it or bought it."

9

The man who emerged from the dirty red import had short dark brown hair, lighter blond eyebrows and moustache and a darker goatee streaked with grey. The woman had shoulder-length dirty blond hair, heavy eyebrows, prominent cheekbones and a receding chin. She wore oversized glasses and was skinnier than any new mother should be. She looked pretty, but haggard.

The man, in an act of touching chivalry, went around to the passenger's side of the car and opened the door. He helped the woman out of the vehicle and on to her feet. She walked with him into her home. In her arms she held a bundle close to her chest.

The man and woman seemed unaware of the net law enforcement cast around their home. As soon as they went inside, the net tightened—and the tension rose. The car looked right. The woman was blonde. And there was a newborn baby. But was it the right baby?

Randy Strong opened his car door and said, "We're going in" to Sheriff Espey. Then, he turned off his cell phone.

In Maryville, Espey struggled to breathe evenly. His mind raced through a catalogue of bad outcomes—a shootout, a hostage-taking, a baby who did not survive the event. He dwelled on the possibility that this lead, too, would be a total dead end—just an innocent couple caring for their own child. He stared at the phone, willing it to ring.

In Melvern, Strong—as instructed by Espey—was the first one at the door. Kevin Montgomery answered the knock and invited them all in. What was going through Kevin's mind as a herd of law enforcement stampeded into his home? Did he, at first, think it must have something to do with his wife's half-brothers, Tommy or Teddy, whom he knew had frequent brushes with the law? Whatever popped into Kevin's head, he was baffled by the intrusion into his home.

As Strong entered the house, he saw Lisa with a newborn baby in her arms. Next to her, he saw the blue glow of a television set. A notice of the Amber Alert for Bobbie Jo's baby scrolled across the bottom of the screen.

Strong asked, "Is that your new baby?"

"Yes," she said. "You want to see it?" Lisa stretched out her arms and handed the baby to Strong. On Lisa's empty hands, a series of small, fresh cuts marked many of her fingers.

When questioned, Kevin related the call from Lisa in Topeka the afternoon before and his drive to pick up her and the baby and bring them both home.

Lisa explained her shopping trip to Topeka that was interrupted when her water broke. She told the officers about the delivery of her baby the day before at the Birth & Women's Center.

While the couple talked to Strong and FBI Special Agent Michael Miller, other members of law enforcement checked out their stories. They learned that no babies were born at the birthing center on December 16.

Since the authorities had all the necessary warrants in hand Strong was able to turn and walk out of the house—with the baby girl still resting in his arms. He activated his cell phone and called Espey. "I have the baby in my hands."

Tears welled in Espey's eyes. As he shared the news with the personnel in the building, the tears flowed—tears of joy for the baby, tears of bitterness for Bobbie Jo. Espey brushed his away and headed out to address the media. Before Espey said a word to the press gathered in Maryville, officers posted outside of the Montgomery home saw media representatives driving past the farmhouse.

Strong stepped off the porch and handed the baby to an agent from the Kansas Bureau of Investigation. The investigator got into his car and rushed the infant to Stormont-Vail Regional Health Center in Topeka for evaluation and DNA testing. Strong returned inside to continue the questioning of the couple in earnest.

Lisa sat with a placid expression plastered across her face as Strong advised her of her constitutional rights. Then he confronted her with the information they learned about the lack of births at the center the day before.

At first, Lisa maintained her original story and Kevin insisted that it all was a big mistake. Why are they hassling us? he wondered. What right do they have to take my baby? His heart raced as he worried that his life was tipping over and he would never be able to set it upright again.

Under the persistence of the questioning, Lisa gave up. Her face sagged, her shoulders slumped. She confessed to strangling Bobbie Jo and removing the fetus with a paring knife she found in Bobbie Jo's kitchen. She admitted that "Abigail" was the Stinnetts' baby—not hers—not Kevin's.

Only one person in the room was surprised—Kevin Montgomery. He felt like he was caught at a carnival on a manic Tilt-A-Whirl. He wanted off this nausea-inducing ride. He wanted to forget the tale his wife just told. It sickened him and confused him. It could not be true. He could not have married, lived with, slept with and trusted his own children to a woman who was capable of committing a crime this awful. This was not the Lisa he married. Not the woman he promised to love, honor and cherish. This was not his life. This was not his world.

Most people who knew Lisa found Kevin's ignorance understandable. They also believed Lisa when she insisted that Kevin knew nothing. A clueless Kevin was a credible image. Lisa had been lying to people—and convincing them of the truth of her falsehoods—all of her life.

10

Lisa Marie Hedberg was born in Washington State on February 27, 1968. Her mother, Judy—born and raised in Kansas with six siblings—moved to the Northwest with her new husband when they got married. Lisa's father, John Hedberg, was a native of Washington and an army man.

When John's new assignment stationed him in Fort Riley, Kansas, the family relocated just west of Topeka. Known as "America's Warfighting Center," Fort Riley had a reputation for excellent training of the armed forces personnel who passed through the base. Built of native limestone, the post's history extended back before the United States Civil War. Brevet Major General George A. Custer commanded the fort after the end of the war and up to the time he commenced his campaign on the high plains. The inconclusive foray resulted in Custer's court martial and one-year suspension from the Army after Custer returned to Fort Riley to see his wife without permission.

During World War II, 125,000 soldiers were trained at these facilities, including heavyweight boxing champion Joe Louis and movie stars like Mickey Rooney. It was still a vital training center with strong relations to the community that surrounded it when John and Judy arrived on base with their baby, Lisa. During the assignment at Fort Riley, their second child, Patty, was born on June 3, 1970.

Lisa was a smart little thing—learning to read by the time she was 4 years old. Reading became a passion for Lisa. She never had time to play with dolls like other little girls. All she wanted to do was read and learn. Her mother said that when her oldest daughter was engrossed in a book, "the house could burn down and she wouldn't even smell the smoke."

The young girl was also obsessed with telling tall tales as the gospel truth. After her mother and father separated, she told everyone she met that her father died in Viet Nam.

After the dissolution of her first marriage, Judy was on her own with two young children. Her little family's standard of living sunk below the poverty level. It was then Judy met a single father of five, Jack Kleiner. He seemed a godsend. She moved with him and his family to Oklahoma.

On June 6, 1974, the number in the household increased by one with the birth of Lisa's first half-brother Teddy. The next year, Jerri was born on June 26, 1975.

In October of that year, Judy and Jack Kleiner were married. Their third and final child, Tommy, was born on April 6, 1978.

Though her lies made everyone in the family angry with her at one time or another, Lisa seemed to thrive. She continued her voracious reading and also learned to play the violin and French horn in grade school. In high school, she played the mellophone in the marching band, making first chair with ease. She acted in a class play and was active in the pep club and student council. She seemed to excel without any discernible effort, racking up A's and B's on her report card.

Beneath the surface of high performance, her mother saw the shadows of trouble to come. At times, Lisa seemed to switch from one personality to another. One moment, she was a sweet, caring child. The next, she was "the daughter of the devil itself." At times, she said, she shrugged it all off as the normal strange phases a child went through growing up. At others, she was afraid of what the future held for her child.

People who knew both Lisa and Judy placed the blame squarely on Judy's doorstep. They said that all her life, Lisa heard her mother telling her that she wasn't good for anything. Judy did not provide Lisa—or any of her children—with any stability, or the security of a mother's unconditional love, one of Lisa's friends insisted.

Her treatment of her children was as mercurial as her moods. As adults, all of Judy's children said that getting along with Mom depended on which way the wind blew. Lisa, a friend said, learned to duck her head when the wind blew the wrong way.

In mid-February of 1983, one of the reasons for Lisa's inner turmoil became apparent to Judy. She came home and walked into a sight that sickened her. She saw her 15-year-old daughter engaged in sexual intercourse with her husband—the girl's stepfather.

Judy was stunned and terrified. Jack threatened to kill her if she told anyone. He was a violent man who had hit and knocked around her and the children for years. She believed he was capable of carrying through on his threat. "At first," she said, "I kept my mouth shut. Then, I told a policeman and he took me to a lawyer."

Even though the inappropriate sexual behavior was going on in her own home for quite some time, Judy claimed she was blind to it. Others argued that claim was a self-protective lie—Judy had known what Jack was doing for years; she simply placed her own well-being over that of her daughter.

Whether her denial of the abuse was subconscious or a deliberate act, when Judy saw it right before her eyes, she could avoid the truth no longer. She confronted Jack, who did not deny it, but still did not express a shred of remorse.

"You can't rape the willing," he said. It was the despicable but typical response of sexual child abusers everywhere. It's heard with sickening frequency on today's news—from the mouths of men like Jack and from female middle school teachers caught in sexual activity with their young adolescent students.

When Judy filed for divorce, Jack claimed in court that his estranged wife made the whole story up to get custody of their children. Judy took Lisa to counseling, but her daughter insisted that she never had sex with her stepfather. Judy had seen it with her own eyes. She knew her daughter was lying.

Lisa confided to others that she denied the abuse for one reason: Jack warned her that if she told anyone about their sexual encounters, he would go after Patty and do the same thing to her. Lisa said she kept her mouth shut to protect her younger sister.

In the summer of 1984, Judy was out on her own again— this time with five children to support and nurture. Jack was failing to make child support proponents and was jailed twice for it. Although the family was now on welfare, Judy said she tried to add an element of fun to their family life with inexpensive excursions—outings at the lake, fishing trips and driving out for ice cream.

Others painted a darker portrait of growing up with Judy. They said she never left one man unless she had another waiting in the wings, and that her children were always secondary to her pursuit of serial monogamy.

Early in 1986, Judy married again. Her third husband was Richard Boman. Richard's children were grown, but his son Carl returned home after a stint in the Navy. The 25-year-old Carl was intrigued by the bright 18-year-old girl now living in his father's house. He expressed his interest to Lisa and the two started dating.

Lisa graduated from high school in the spring of that year. She planned to join the Air Force to get money for college.

Then she learned she was pregnant. Her plans for furthering her education were abandoned. She and Carl married in August 1986, in Cleveland, Oklahoma.

Lisa was not the only child impacted by the tumultuous life with Judy and a series of stepfathers. Every one of Judy's children had a run-in with the law. Except for Lisa, all of them experimented to some extent with illegal drugs. For some reason, Lisa never attempted to escape from the realities of her life with an artificial high. Patty now claimed she was the only one of Judy's children to never spend a night in jail.

Judy did not provide them with a good template for healthy relationships, and that was demonstrated in the way they interacted with each other. They were fierce in the defense of a sibling when anyone outside the family launched an attack. Within their circle, however, they were ruthless. They never hesitated to step on one of their own in a series of never-ending power plays.

Each of the kids had reasons for resenting Judy. All grew up and moved away. Yet, somehow, they all found themselves drawn back to her side—compelled to be near her to perpetuate the warped family equation.

11

Lisa entered her marriage to Carl in 1986 torn between emulating the mother she loved and pushing away from the mom she resented. She longed for normalcy, stability and security, and yet she still followed her mother's path.

In less than four years, Lisa had three daughters and a son. Desiree Nichole was born in 1987, Chelsea Lynne in 1988, Carl James Boman II—who everyone called C.J.—in 1989 and Kayla Deanna in 1990. After the birth of the fourth child, Lisa underwent a tubal ligation procedure under pressure from her husband to ensure that baby was her last. This frenzied bout of procreation foreshadowed the desperation that would possess Lisa once she was unable to have any more children. As long as she stayed pregnant, she felt confident that Carl would not leave no matter how serious their marital problems became.

Carl worked long hours to meet the high financial demands

of his family of six. Lisa stayed home to care for the children and the housekeeping.

But Lisa did not live up to her part of the bargain. The house was filthy and roach-infested. She was known to feed lunch to her children, on at least one occasion, by setting a cold casserole dish of leftovers on the floor in front of them while they played. She preferred to spend her time stretched out on the sofa reading. Her favorite books were novels by Stephen King.

Her lackadaisical attitude toward the maintenance of the family home drove Carl to distraction and spawned endless rounds of marital spats. According to family lore, as Lisa's marriage deteriorated, she made a bad situation even worse by traipsing off for wild flings—leaving her family for days or even weeks. Once she even showed up at a family reunion with another man.

One of Lisa's friends contradicted that version of events, saying that Carl was the one who cheated on Lisa—again and again. He also battered his wife on a regular basis, she said.

Whoever was violating their wedding vows, Carl had enough of the marriage. He filed for divorce in October 1993. He moved to Springdale, Arkansas—a town of 46,000 just north of Fayetteville on Interstate 540. Nestled in the northwest corner of the state in the Ozark Mountains, Springdale was surrounded by a lush, natural beauty. It was difficult to decide which season was the most glorious time of year there—spring with its explosive rebirth of brilliant green or autumn with the variegated splendor of turning foliage.

Springdale was an embarkation point for scenic train trips through the Ozark Mountains, the corporate headquarters for chicken giant Tyson Foods and the home of the Shiloh Museum of Ozark History. The museum was dedicated to the development of an understanding and appreciation of the history of northwest Arkansas. The collections in its six historical buildings included 400,000 photographic images of life in the six-county region.

Carl was states away now, but Lisa was not ready to give

up on her marriage yet. She packed up the kids and followed him to his new home.

At the end of 1993, Lisa looked Carl in the eye and said that she was pregnant with a fifth child. It was the perfect way to manipulate him, and she knew it. Carl was aware that she'd had her tubes tied at his request, but he also knew that, on occasion, the procedure failed.

As a family, they attended the Fayetteville Reorganized Church of Jesus Christ of the Latter Day Saints on Old Wire Road in Springdale. The denomination was an offshoot of the traditional Salt Lake City–based Mormon Church that had split from the home body over the election of Brigham Young as church leader more than a century before. In 2002, this Independence, Missouri–based denomination of 250,000 members in fifty countries changed their name to the Community of Christ.

Through the Church, the divorced couple worked on their relationship. For a couple interested in healing their family, their choice of congregation made sense. Although the Church had deep historical roots in polygamy, it now embraced monogamy as the basic principle of marriage. Solidarity of the family was a basic tenet of the faithful. The teachings led them to strengthen family ties through mutual respect and the building of healthy relationships.

Unfortunately, their definition of marriage did not include the concept of equal rights for women—an absence that fed into Lisa's feelings of worthlessness outside of her role as mother. The philosophy of equality between the sexes was considered disruptive to family life by the Church.

The counseling and fellowship achieved the desired goal for Carl and Lisa. Eight months after they started attending the church, they remarried in a service there on June 11, 1994.

The 1993 pregnancy vanished into thin air. It was a new year and Lisa was telling her family that she was pregnant again—this time with twins. Carl knew the only place the pregnancy existed was in Lisa's own mind. Her mother,

Judy, doubted it was possible. She'd been at the hospital with Lisa when she had her tubes tied. She believed her daughter was lying again.

Carl, Lisa and the four children then moved to Deming, New Mexico. Carl claimed the move was initiated by Lisa, who could not bear to stick around Springdale after months passed and no birth was forthcoming. Carl's father, Richard, owned a double-wide trailer there, and the young Boman family moved in and made a fresh start.

Deming was located in the southwest corner of New Mexico—west of Las Cruces and El Paso, Texas—just off of Interstate 10. It was the seat of Luna County, the "Chile capital of the world" where the long growing season made a success of crops like green and red chilies, melons, pecans, cotton and a variety of grains and vegetables.

In the early 1800s, Deming was such a rough place that outlaws rounded up in Arizona were given a one-way ticket to Deming as punishment. Many now were glad to call Deming home. Surrounded by wide-open spaces, clean air, mountains, high desert and panoramic views, Deming was a place where the sunshine was nearly constant and cacti sprout on every bare patch of ground. Because of its high elevation, warm summer days were tempered by comfortable nights, clear skies dominated the winter months and humidity was low year round.

The beauty and bounty of colorful desert rocks in and around Deming earned it the moniker of a "Rock-Hunters Paradise." It was a small town compared to the Bomans' last home in Springdale. Deming's population was just over 14,000. The stark landscape was in sharp contrast to the endless green wildness of the Ozark Mountain home they left behind.

Carl worked as a delivery man for a restaurant, the Desert Inn. Lisa got a job working for the local newspaper, *The Headlight*, as an inserter and route supervisor. The periodical was published Monday through Friday and had a daily circulation of 3,700.

At home, Lisa raised chickens and goats. She taught all of her children how to weave, dye and spin the wool she harvested from the goats. She had boundless reserves of energy for pursuit of this back-to-the-earth hobby.

Her poor household habits, however, showed no sign of improvement. Carl's supervisor, Bill Boomhower, said, "You could barely walk through the place. The only time the place got clean was when Carl did it. Teachers at the Sunshine School would take care of the children and bring in clean clothes for them."

"Lisa was very quiet," Bill said. "She didn't have a lot of friends."

Monica Gutierrez, Lisa's coworker at *The Headlight* told reporters, "She loved her kids. She was always with them. She was always worried about them."

Unlike most of the others at the newspaper, Monica was willing to listen with sympathy to Lisa's endless litany of problems. "She'd get in trouble with management because she'd be talking. She couldn't focus on her work."

She obviously could not focus on nurturing her marriage, either. In 1998, it ended. Lisa had no more tricks up her sleeve to hold it together. She knew she could no longer claim pregnancy and bind Carl to her side. He was awake and aware—he saw her lies coming before they crossed her lips.

Carl left with all four children and settled in Bartlesville, Oklahoma. Lisa filed divorce papers in Deming on June 30. Carl was served on July 3. The marriage was over for good.

The Sixth Judicial District Court in Luna County granted the divorce on August 6. The ruling gave joint custody of the children to both parents, but granted physical custody to Lisa and visitation rights to Carl.

Once the legal process was behind her, Lisa moved to Kansas to live with her mother. By then, Judy and Richard Boman had divorced, too. Judy had a new husband, Danny Shaughnessy. They lived on a farm outside of the town of Lyndon—population 1,038. There they raised cows, geese,

chickens, pigs, sheep and goats. They made their own
sausage, tended a strawberry patch and cultivated a large
vegetable garden. They did everything they could to live off
the land.

According to one of Lisa's friends, Judy built up a negative reputation with many in her community. Most of the
time, it was easy to get along with her. Then, for no discernible reason, she'd flip. Without warning, a few women
who thought she was a friend were startled to hear outrageous stories about themselves blanketing the community—
all handwoven by Judy Shaughnessy.

In Kansas in 1999, Lisa Boman met Kevin Montgomery.
In a few short years, she tore his normal small-town world
apart.

12

Melvern, Kansas, just off of Interstate Highway 35 between Kansas City and Wichita, was settled in 1868. Not many people knew that the town was named after the Malvern Hills in Scotland—a nine-mile-long landmark that humped above the flat Malvern Plain. An unfortunate error in the original town filing spelled the name with an "e" instead of an "a"—and obscured the connection between the two places. The hills across the ocean were filled with prehistoric sites and were home of one of this new town's founders.

By 1871, Melvern consisted of 100 people living in twenty houses, along with a small sawmill, three dry goods stores, a drugstore and a blacksmith shop. The town didn't grow until rail arrived in the mid-1880s. At that point, the population soared to 491 and remained fairly stable thereafter.

Many small towns the size of Melvern went into a spiral of decay and ennui in the social upheaval of the 1960s and never recovered. Fortunately for this small village, there were folks who cared enough to make plans for improvement and follow through on their commitments.

In 1988, thirty folks gathered for a town hall meeting at the local extension office. They divided into five or six work groups and got busy ascertaining the town's needs. The two top items on the list were a grocery store and a community building. They couldn't do much about a private enterprise, but they got busy fulfilling their dream of a community center in 2000, accumulating money with a series of fundraisers. When they reached $30,000, they found out about the possibility of funding through the KAN STEP program in the state's commerce department and secured a $340,000 grant.

It was an awesome accomplishment for a town of its size, but the people of Melvern did not stop there. Next, they tackled Jones Park.

The Jones brothers passed away in the 1950s, leaving behind the Jones Fund as their legacy. Initially, the money was used to provide college scholarships and meet medical expenses for needy families in a three-county area. As the funds grew, the mission expanded in the 60s to include grants for parks and other recreational sites. At that time, money was provided to establish a basic park in the center of Melvern.

It was a nice green space, but lacked any amenities. In the 90s, the townspeople wanted more. They presented a proposal to add a playground and restrooms to the park and received a $50,000 matching grant from the Jones Fund. After four months of donated labor and additional monetary contributions from the citizens of the town, they had a created a cheerful spot in the middle of town. Colorful jungle gyms, slides and swings for the children added a brightness and vivacity to the downtown area.

Projects like these provided more than an aesthetic lift. They also revitalized the town spirit and defeated the dreariness found in many small rural towns. Instead of a glum giving-up attitude, visitors were greeted with the upbeat energy of a small vital community.

Kevin's parents, Roger and Joy Montgomery, moved to Melvern in the early 70s. Roger, an electrician, was drawn to the area by the promise of work on the development of Melvern Lake.

The lake in the Marais Des Cygnes River Basin was one of a network of Army Corps of Engineer projects authorized by the United States Congress in the 50s to reduce flood damage and enhance water resources. It was situated on over 23,000 acres of federally owned land—the footprint of the lake itself covered nearly 7,000 of those acres.

Melvern felt like home to the Montgomerys after the completion of that project, and the family dug its roots deeper and stayed. Roger found a new job at the Wolf Creek Generating Station in neighboring Coffey County. The nuclear plant was a pressurized water reactor providing 1,200,000 kilowatts of energy daily.

Roger and Joy were active in the community, helping to make the difference that was so clear to see on a drive through town. They were an instrumental force in the construction of the community building and in the improvements to Jones Park. Their son, Kevin, also donated his labor to the cause.

Kevin and Lisa met when they worked together in Topeka. He was a family-oriented man who unlike Lisa, came from a functional, intact home. The attraction was mutual—the love of kids a shared value. They began dating soon after their first encounter.

In 1999, the relationship was still quite new when Lisa pulled one of her old tricks out of the bag and informed Kevin that she was pregnant. If she had hoped to coerce a wedding proposal with this news, she was sorely mistaken—the wounds from a bitter divorce were still too fresh for Kevin. He gave her the money to get an abortion. Lisa pocketed the cash, but never got the procedure—there wasn't any need.

Then she concocted another pregnancy tale to stir up
Kevin's sympathy. She confessed that she'd gotten pregnant
when she was a teenager. She carried the baby full term, she
said, but after the delivery—no baby. Everyone told her that
the infant was born dead—but that was just a horrible trick.

Her baby had survived, she told Kevin. Behind her back,
her own mother put the baby up for adoption. Years later, her
suspicions that her family duped her became more certain in
her mind. She investigated and tracked down the baby's
adoptive parents, discovering that her oldest biological child
was named Sarah.

There is no indication that any part of this story was true.

Kevin, though, accepted everything Lisa told him without
question. He took her at face value and believed her version
of any event over that of everyone else. He was a quiet,
clean-cut guy who accepted life the way it was—preferring
to go along to get along, rather than challenge much of anything.

Kevin married Lisa in March 2000. People who knew
him were surprised that he was willing to jump into another
commitment so soon after his messy separation from his
first wife. But he took the leap and soon had not only a new
wife but a bunch of new children and the responsibility that
went with it.

The newlyweds moved with Lisa's three daughters and
son to a rural farmhouse in Osage County just outside
Melvern. The first house was small and crowded for this
family of six. On weekends, when Kevin's three boys came
from their mother's home to visit their dad, the place was
jammed tighter than a skyscraper elevator at quitting time.

In September 2001, they rented a larger farmhouse from
Isabel Phelon. To get to their new home, Kevin and Lisa followed State Route 31 as it cut through downtown Melvern,
then turned left and headed out to Melvern Lake. After a
small cluster of houses, the landscape opened to rolling
fields—acre after acre of land that grew soybeans, milo,
wheat and corn, or raised head after head of cattle. Lines of

trees marched down the fence lines and along the roadways.

A little ways outside of town was the Melvern Cemetery. Old and new markers filled the little plot of land wedged between plowed and fallow fields. The stones from the 1800s were worn smooth by the wind, the rain, the snow—and splotched with rusty moss-like stains. It required squinted eyes and sensitive fingers to decipher the names and dates engraved on their faces.

Just a bit beyond the graveyard was the gravel and dirt of South Adams Road. Gravel crunched under tires as the road rose up over a hump and crossed two sets of railroad tracks. Finally, it arrived at the home of Lisa and Kevin Montgomery—1.8 miles and five doors from the highway.

Their new home—in traditional farmhouse white—was set back from the road just far enough to escape the pings of flying gravel. The side facing the street was a two-story rectangle. A one-story structure with a sloping roof covering a broad porch stuck out behind it. A barn and other outbuildings were scattered nearby, and well-used fields surrounded the three sides not bound by the road.

Past their house and down a small hill, the road reached an intersection. Just around that corner was the home of their landlady. The roofline was visible from the porch.

Kevin commuted up this bumpy road and seventy miles farther to get to work at Acme Sign in Kansas City, Missouri. The company was owned by Melvern native Darrell Schultze. There, Kevin used his electrician background in his work as a sign fabricator. He was a very particular and meticulous worker—more interested in doing his job right than in completing the task in record time.

The family threw themselves into the rural lifestyle. They raised their own hogs for meat for the dinner table. When time came to send off one of them for slaughter, Kevin's boss, Darrell, often came by to help Lisa load the animal onto the truck. The Montgomerys raised a calf or two each year as well. Their livestock included a small herd of angora goats. She wanted to teach her children all she knew about

the down-to-earth skills of gardening, cooking and raising
livestock.

She sheared her goats and washed and dried the wool.
Then the kids picked through it and carded the soft hair. This
was the most tedious step in the process. The children soon
learned to hide from sight when wool cleaning time came
around.

When that chore was done, Lisa spun the wool into yarn,
picking out any little pieces of grass or burrs that the children missed. She wrote for advice online:

> I am hoping to learn how to knit a pair of socks with
> some of it, but my kids have already asked for mit-
> tens! Since it is white, I should be able to dye it, so
> here is another question—is it better to dye the
> wool or the already spun yarn? Or does it matter?
> And what are some natural dyes that I can find
> around a farm that would work?

Lisa loved the Internet. She posted online about her children and what she would do differently with the kids she
would have with Kevin:

> I had four kids a year apart. They learned coopera-
> tion, manners and are closer than they were be-
> fore. As they are all in high school now, we have
> plans when they all graduate that our next ones will
> be home-schooled the first couple of years.

To the people of Melvern, Lisa always seemed to be pregnant. They lost count of the number of miscarriages she
claimed. In one incident, she told everyone that she donated
the lost fetus to science.

The Montgomerys' minister, Reverend Mike Wheatley
of the First Church of God, later said that Kevin and Lisa
wanted their own children. Of course, Lisa never bothered
to tell Kevin about the tubal ligation she had years before

she met him. She hid her sterility and Kevin was none the wiser. Lisa told her preacher that when she and Kevin had a child of their own, she would be "attached at the hip to her husband."

"There was a desperation there," Wheatley told the media.

Wheatley and his wife thought Lisa was a very self-centered person who at the same time appeared to care deeply about her family and her kids. When they tried to talk to her about anything else, it was impossible.

Often Lisa dropped by the parsonage with her children. Whenever the Wheatleys turned the conversation to someone else in their congregation, Lisa either ignored their comments or cut them off and continued to talk only about her little world.

13

In 2002, Lisa started breeding rat terriers. By June 2003, she had three dogs in her kennel and was active on the rat terrier boards online. It was through these chat rooms that she encountered Jason Dawson, another rat terrier enthusiast who lived in the Kansas City area. Lisa had a male dog that Jason wanted to breed with one of his females. The two met at the Great Mall of the Great Plains in Olathe, Kansas—the halfway point between their homes.

Jason met with Lisa on two other occasions. Once, he brought one of his males to breed with Lisa's female. On another occasion, Jason brought two puppies to Lisa for transport to another breeder at a dog show in Lexington, Kentucky.

Lisa made him uncomfortable at every encounter. "There was something just plain odd about her, but I couldn't put my finger on it," he said.

Nonetheless, he did not break contact with her until he

became aware of her propensity for telling silly, unnecessary lies. When breeder Nancy Strudl accused Lisa of misrepresenting the pedigree of the dogs she sold, many in the rat terrier community were outraged and wanted Lisa ousted from their group. Only one person came to Lisa's defense—a respected young breeder named Bobbie Jo Stinnett. "Maybe it was just a misunderstanding," she wrote. She urged others to give Lisa a second chance. Because of their high regard for Bobbie Jo, the others relented.

Jason also learned of Lisa's bizarre machinations over a puppy she got from one Tracey Ramirez. Lisa said she kept the dog when she actually gave it away. She then went to visit the animal and take photographs of it as it grew up. She sent these snapshots to Tracy to perpetuate the myth that the animal still lived with her.

As one deception piled on another, Jason put distance between himself and Lisa. He did not plan to interact with her again. When he did, he would not be aware that it was Lisa—he thought it was another person altogether.

Lisa was also involved in the lives of the children in her family. She attended school plays, worked with the kids in their 4-H club and always showed up for Little League games. She often was seen on the sidelines—one eye on the game, another on her busy fingers as she knitted away. She sewed pioneer-style outfits for her daughters and nieces to deck them out for the annual apple festival.

The kids went to class at the Marais Des Cygnes school on Main Street in Melvern, which housed both elementary and high school classes.

Lisa worked away from home, too. At one point, she juggled three jobs simultaneously: at Wendy's on Interstate 35, at the Greyhound bus stop in Topeka, and at Casey's General Store and gas station in Lyndon.

She enjoyed her job at Casey's. She was friendly to all the customers and well-liked by the regulars. She developed a friendship with the woman she worked with on the weekend.

Her coworker thought Lisa was very easy to get to know. It was comfortable to talk to Lisa—and they talked a lot. Often, they exchanged stories about their children, who were about the same ages. Lisa, she said, loved her kids and took a lot of pride in their accomplishments.

She never expressed any concerns about them except for the garden variety complaints that all parents make. She seemed to have a good relationship with all of her children. The people of Melvern liked them, too. One after another, they described Lisa's children as "four of the sweetest kids you'll ever meet." Lisa was particularly excited about Kayla's interest in rat terriers and dog shows.

While working together throughout 2004, the two women often discussed the progress of Lisa's pregnancy. The coworker commiserated with Lisa about her morning sickness and her swelling feet.

The deepest, most heartfelt conversations they had revolved around Lisa's mother, Judy Shaughnessy. Lisa expressed a fervent desire to forgive her mother, but actually doing it seemed a nearly insurmountable challenge.

On the surface, hearing Lisa list her activities was like reading the résumé of Super-Mom. Down deep, though, a deadly desperation was building. It manifested itself in the lies about her pregnancy. She displayed it, too, in her interactions with her half-brother Teddy and his girlfriend, Bonnie Taylor. Once Teddy's son, Justin, was born, Lisa constantly badgered the couple to give the child to her.

Her desire to remove Justin from the care of Teddy and Bonnie did have merit. On a wind-whipped bitter cold day, the couple had been seen hitching rides along the highway with their baby in tow. The little child had to be suffering—wrapped in the thinnest of blankets and exposed to the cold.

On July 22, 2003, just before the baby's first birthday, authorities from the Drug Enforcement Unit descended on Teddy and Bonnie's home on East 8th Street in Ottawa, Kansas. Teddy was charged with one count for the possession of methamphetamine; three counts related to the manufacture of it; one count for the possession of ephedrine, pseudoephed-rine, red phosphorous, lithium metal, sodium metal and other substances considered precursors of the controlled substance; a felony drug paraphernalia possession charge for the coffee filters, plastic tubing, acetone, matchbooks, phosphorous acid flakes, Red Devil Lye, aluminum foil, muriatic acid, Coleman Fuel and other items used in the processing, testing and distri-bution of a controlled substance; and a misdemeanor charge for possession of syringes and a spoon.

Because he was a first-time felony offender, he was able to get a reduced-term plea agreement. Only two prior misde-meanor incidents were on his record—both in Oklahoma: a driving with a suspended license charge in August 1999 and the unlawful possession of marijuana and resisting an officer on May 7, 2002.

Teddy pled guilty and received a sentence of 6 years in the El Dorado Correctional Facility, followed by 3 years of probation on the manufacturing charges plus an additional 13 months in prison on the possession charge. This short sentence was a departure from the federal drug guidelines, which called for incarceration for a 12½-year minimum on the manufacturing charge alone.

Many believed the only reason Teddy got caught and arrested in the first place was that Lisa tipped off the author-ities and sent them to her half-brother's door. With Teddy behind bars, her plot to get custody of her young nephew moved forward.

Two days after Teddy's arrest, Lisa, her sister Patty Baldwin and her half-brother Tommy Kleiner were at Teddy's house. Tommy was there at the request of his mother to pick up a microwave oven and some dishes that Judy loaned to the now incarcerated couple.

After loading up his car with his mother's things, Tommy could not get his engine to start. He raised the hood and pulled out a knife to scrape the corrosive buildup off of the battery terminals.

Lisa and Patty came outside, Lisa calling Tommy's name. He pulled his head out from under the hood with the knife in hand. Lisa saw the sunlight glisten on the blade and recognized a golden opportunity for drama. She taunted Tommy and accused him of threatening her. Lisa's performance goaded Tommy into further action. He waved the knife around in the air, gave Patty a shove and shouted threats to both of the women. Lisa shrieked and the two sisters ran inside. Lisa called 9-1-1. Lisa told the responding officers that Tommy threatened to slice her throat with a knife.

While Lisa was on the phone, Tommy started his car and drove back to Lyndon in neighboring Osage County. According to his mother, Judy, Tommy drove to her farm. She said that DEA agents—thinking that Tommy might be connected to Teddy's drug business—surrounded Judy's home. They entered the house and removed Tommy at gunpoint.

Official records paint a different picture of that day's events. Tommy was actually arrested at his own home in downtown Lyndon. There were no federal agents involved at all. Tommy was taken into custody and transferred to Franklin County.

Judy, it seemed, had once again colored reality with the story she wanted to tell in contradiction of the actual series of events.

Authorities charged Tommy with two felony counts of making violent threats with the intent to terrorize and one misdemeanor count of domestic battery for hostile physical contact with Patty Baldwin.

Tommy had a string of misdemeanor convictions in his past, but no felonies. In August 2000, he received a 10-day sentence, a year of probation and mandatory alcohol/drug education after he was found guilty of driving under the influence, improper driving on a paved road and racing on highways.

He had to pay a $500 fine and was sentenced to 90 days behind bars with another year of probation for misdemeanor battery against a law enforcement officer in November 2002.

While still on the stretch of probation, he was busted again.

He pled *nolo contendere* to charges that he obstructed a process server and for criminal damage to property when he kicked in a patrol car window. He had to pay court costs, fees and restitution totaling $684. His two 90-day sentences for the offenses were stayed in exchange for an additional 6-month supervised probationary period. During that time, he was required to attend anger management classes, receive a mental health evaluation and make regular monthly payments.

In September, the current felony charges involving his half-sisters were reduced to misdemeanors. Tommy received a 60-day suspended sentence with a year of probation. He paid $177 in court costs and was ordered to continue counseling and to have no contact with Lisa Montgomery. There was no restraining order issued on behalf of Patty Baldwin because she did not seek one. She sent a short handwritten letter to the court: "I, Patty Baldwin, am requesting that the 'no contact order' for my brother Tommy Kleiner be lifted. I do not agree with the charges that the state has filed against him." Although she was upset at the time of the incident, she no longer saw it as a big deal at all—and she was upset with Lisa for not letting it all go.

But Lisa still thought it was a big deal. Tommy only served one day behind bars and Lisa was not satisfied. According to Tommy and Lisa's mother, she followed Tommy around and then reported him for violating the restraining order.

However, the report Officer Stout of the Lyndon police turned in told a different story. Lisa was at work at Casey's General Store on the afternoon of November 30. Tommy and his girlfriend, Adrienne Von Behren, entered the store. Tommy picked up an item, went to the counter, threw down some money and left.

Lisa turned to Adrienne and said, "I'm calling the police."

"Please do," Adrienne said. "He came in here on purpose."

One of Lisa's friends insisted that Adrienne sided with

Lisa because her relationship with Tommy was temporary—
a month-long fling in the middle of Tommy's relationship
with another woman.

Why either woman was interested in Tommy was a big
question. When he and his regular girlfriend finally broke up
for good, they both went to court and obtained mutual restraining orders.

Lisa and Adrienne's story was contradicted by a man who
was pumping gas when it all came down. He said Tommy
never entered the store at all. He just pulled in, filled up his
truck and drove away.

The authorities may not have been able to discern the
truth, but they nonetheless filed a motion to revoke Tommy's probation. While it was pending, Lisa filed another
complaint that Tommy was in violation of the restraining
order.

On December 13, Jeremiah Tull drove Tommy to the Citizens State Bank in Lyndon. Both men went inside. While
they were there, Lisa arrived at the bank. There was no communication between Lisa and Tommy, and Tommy left as
soon as he finished his business there. Lisa accused him of
stalking her, but the version of events as portrayed by bank-
ing personnel gave more credence to Judy's claim that Lisa
was following Tommy.

Tommy's anger management group leader, Fred Eles-
land, wrote a positive report on Tommy's progress to his attorney, who submitted it to the court. He wrote:

> Tommy Kleiner has completed one course of anger man-
> agement at this agency and recently asked if he can come
> back for more therapy due to another incident with an-
> other agency for which he needs to go to court.
>
> [. . .] He has indicated that seeing me has been help-
> ful. When I first met him he was reacting negatively to
> almost every interaction he had with authority figures.
> I'm afraid he still has problems with them but, at least
> now, he is more apt to take a time out and cool off rather

than respond in a negative way and be arrested. It seems to me that this is progress.

I like him. He is very open with his feelings and I have the feeling that I can confront him openly and can challenge him to respond in ways that aren't going to get him into further trouble.

Despite this letter and regardless of the questionable integrity of Lisa's testimony, on February 11, 2004, the court found Tommy violated the no-contact provision of his suspended sentence and sent him to jail to serve the remaining 57 days of his sentence.

In the fall of 2003, Lisa was wearing maternity clothes again. She chattered to everyone who would listen about the upcoming birth of her baby. This pregnancy was conceived as part of Lisa's ramp-up campaign to wrestle possession of her half-brother's child, Justin, from her mother, Judy. Authorities had placed the boy in foster care when they arrested Teddy and his girlfriend.

Before the day of the hearing, Judy assumed she would have no trouble gaining custody of her grandchild. She had serious doubts when Lisa stepped into the courtroom. Lisa faced the judge clad in the apparel of an expectant mother. She argued that, as a mother-to-be, she was a better choice for rearing a small child. The final decision on Justin's fate was continued to a second hearing.

Waiting for that day in court, Lisa's due date grew near. She discarded her maternity clothing and claimed she had a miscarriage. In the next hearing, Lisa mournfully explained to the judge that she lost the baby at six months and donated the unborn child's body to science. She believed her loss and sacrifice would force the court's hand. The judge, however, was not moved by her pregnancy at the first hearing and was not moved by sympathy for her loss in this one. The court awarded custody of Justin Kleiner to his grandmother Judy.

Lisa did find sympathy at the First Church of God. The

congregation wrapped around her in fellowship. They prayed for her as she grieved over her miscarriage. They shed tears on her behalf.

Soon after her failure to get the child, Lisa gave birth to her plan to buy a baby. She heard a rumor that her ex-husband's new wife, Vanessa, was coming into an inheritance from her father. She contacted Carl and Vanessa demanding $45,000 in cash.

When they denied her request, she badgered them again and again. On one occasion, she even threatened to "destroy" Vanessa. Vanessa later told the London *Mail*: "We were really concerned about what was going to happen because we couldn't afford to give her the money even if we'd wanted to. I was convinced she was going to do something dreadful, and I thought Carl and I were in danger."

Later in 2004, Patty ran into her sister at the Whistle Stop Cafe in Lyndon. Lisa lifted up her shirt, grabbed Patty's hand and placed it on her distended belly. "Feel it. Feel it," she said.

Patty was confused. She knew Lisa couldn't be pregnant, but all the same, she knew that her abdomen was as hard as if she were.

Despite the physical evidence, Lisa's family knew she was lying again. Kevin and his family, on the other hand, believed every word. In December, Lisa's sister Patty decided to intervene and set the record straight. She went to Lisa's home. She brushed past her sister and confronted Kevin. "Your wife cannot be pregnant because she had a tubal ligation in 1990."

Lisa ordered Patty to leave her home and never come back.

A week later, Judy and Jerri visited Kevin's parents, Roger and Joy Montgomery. Judy explained Lisa's long history of falsehoods and said, "Lisa is fooling you again."

Although warned, the Montgomery family did not put any credibility in the allegations made by Lisa's family. Lisa had been busy since her marriage poisoning the minds of her husband's family against her own. The Montgomerys did not understand why Lisa's mother and sisters wanted to hurt her, but they took Lisa's word that they did.

Judy told Lisa, "You cannot keep lying to this man. He doesn't deserve it."

Lisa plotted her revenge. First, she attempted to get a restraining order prohibiting her mother and sister from seeing her children. When that didn't work, she filed a court order to stop them from telling people that she faked pregnancies.

Judy was concerned enough about Lisa's mental stability that she consulted attorneys about getting Lisa into a psychiatric institution. She felt it was the only option that would prevent her daughter from spiralling out of control. She was told by her lawyer, though, that unless Lisa harmed herself or someone else, there were no legal grounds for an involuntary commitment.

In the midst of all of this family turmoil, Lisa went to a dog show with her daughter Kayla. It was a cold and rainy venue. It was the first face-to-face meeting between Lisa and Bobbie Jo Stinnett, a small-town girl from Skidmore, Missouri. But it would not be the last.

14

The town of Skidmore was founded when Marteny Skidmore moved from Virginia to Missouri and purchased 700 acres of land in the Nodaway River Valley. By 1880, it had a population of 400. On December 29, 1886, the first town newspaper—the *Skidmore Advance*—rolled off the presses. The motto on its masthead read: "To publish a paper and make money."

Skidmore was small, but it was proud and determined to etch out its own distinct identity. There was no better way to draw attention in the rural countryside of northwest Missouri than with a yearly event that attracted visitors from miles around.

The annual Punkin Show—a tradition that lasted more than a century—began on October 17, 1899. The first year, it was a one-day show. In time it expanded to a four-day event. Produce, handiwork, crafts and baked goods were judged. Special entertainment—from biplane rides to dances—livened up life in the small town.

The town initiated a second annual event in 1988 to commemorate veterans—Freedom Fest. This event drew visitors from thirty states. Every year, it featured food and craft vendors and a live bald eagle named Moose provided by Operation Wildlife out of Linwood, Kansas. The organizers tried to bring back crowd favorites and find new unique entertainment each year.

Large-scale living history exhibitions including re-enactments of military drills were a big draw for the children in attendance. A Civil War–era baseball game brought a new dimension to the all-American sport. Special speakers included Adrian Cronauer, author of *Good Morning, Vietnam*, John Burnam, a dog handler in the Vietnam War and Dorinda Nicholson, who as a child witnessed the bombing of Pearl Harbor.

To raise money to cover the basic expenses, the organizers auctioned homemade pies. In 2005, a new fundraising event was added before the event—flamingoing. People associated with the event snuck into the yards of neighbors to plant a flock of plastic flamingoes. To have the pink birds removed, homeowners made a $5 contribution to Freedom Fest. For another five bucks, that person could designate the next home to be invaded by the flock.

Demand was greater than anticipated. The waiting list was long—filled with people who wanted the flock to visit their own homes, and others who wanted them to land in a friend's yard. Organizers had to invest in a second flock to meet demand and get the flock to every yard on the list before the celebration began. Patriotic sentiment, homemade pies and family fun—nothing was more symbolic of the heartland of America than that. Co-organizer Cheryl Huston said, "If you didn't love America when you got here, you will when you leave."

Skidmore, situated at the junction of Missouri Highway 113 and Route DD, was surrounded by endless acres of rolling farmland. Dusty gravel roads wended past large white farm-houses, weathered barns and fields of soybeans.

In the year of Bobbie Jo's birth, the population of her home town was 437. Since then, Skidmore had wasted away. By 2004, only 320 folks called it home.

At the heart of town—the intersection known as Newton's corner—Skidmore sagged with weariness. A sense of ennui went beyond the occupied buildings with their flaky paint and sagging gutters—past the vacant structures whose blinded, grime-caked windows were desperate for a swipe of ammonia water—and deep into the pores of the community.

In some ways, the downsizing of this small town was similar to what was happening all across rural Missouri. In Skidmore, though, it seemed more extreme and more mind-numbing. One quarter of the population was gone, the doors to its only elementary school closed in 2001 and many of its businesses shuttered for good. The annual Skidmore Punkin Show was cancelled for the first time in 2004 due to lack of interest. The worn water tower bearing the town's name loomed over Skidmore like a prescient tombstone.

Still, Skidmore—and all of northwest Missouri—was a safe place to raise a family with rock-solid Midwestern values grounded in a sense of community and belonging that was as natural to the residents as the dirt beneath their feet. The rate of crime in the county was low. In the year 2000, only 317 crimes were reported, and two-thirds of those were for larceny charges. Only one was murder. Only one was rape.

Somehow, though, many of the crimes in Nodaway County seemed to have a peculiarity about them that made them stand out from the bare statistics. In 1930, 20-year-old Velma Colter was a teacher at the Garrett School, a little white country schoolhouse with only a handful of students. On December 16, she was raped and beaten to death at her place of work.

Before Christmas, authorities arrested a black ex-convict named Raymond Gunn. He confessed to the murder after he was behind bars. A group of men planned to remove Gunn from official custody and administer their idea of swift justice. Sheriff Havre English heard about the plot and moved Gunn down to jail in St. Joseph for his safety before trial.

The prisoner was returned to the Nodaway County Jail in time to attend his January 12 arraignment. When Sheriff English attempted to transport Gunn from the prison to the courthouse, he was overwhelmed by a large angry mob— estimates placed the number of people at somewhere between 800 to 3,000. They marched the handcuffed Gunn away from the authorities and out of town—down three miles of road to the place where Velma had died.

Their thirst for vengeance intensified with each step they took, and their number grew with every passing minute. People from surrounding Missouri towns and even some from across the state line in Iowa gathered at the Garrett School.

Gunn begged for his life all along the route of his forced death march. Instead of soothing the crowd or bringing it to its senses, his appeals to their mercy and humanity inflamed their passions even more. By the time the front of the mob escorting Gunn arrived at the schoolhouse, lines of incoming participants stretched out in lines a mile long in all four directions.

A group of men formed a tight circle around Gunn, taunting and battering him as others raced inside the school in search of a ladder. When it was found, they propped it up on the side of the school building.

Men dragged Gunn up the rungs to the rooftop. Angry hands ripped off shingles to expose the rafters beneath. Chains wrapped around the beams and around the terrified Raymond Gunn.

On the ground, frenzied men siphoned gasoline from the cars at the scene. A chain of men passed the containers of lethal liquid from hand to hand across the schoolyard and up the ladder. On the roof, other men splashed the flammable liquid on the loose shingles, on the exposed beams and on the body of the black man accused—but not convicted—of raping and murdering a white woman.

Gunn pulled his body into as tight a ball as the chains would allow. The match was lit. The flames soared. Smoke swirled into the country sky. One witness said that Gunn had passed out before the pyre was lit. Another said Gunn waved to the crowd before he died. But no one was deaf to his wails of agony. And everyone inhaled the reek of gasoline fumes and the stench of burning flesh.

After ten minutes of burning, the roof collapsed. The remains of Raymond Gunn fell down into the school and landed on top of a desk in the classroom below.

In Maryville, sixty National Guardsmen stood at the ready awaiting orders to leave the armory. Those orders never came.

Thousands of participants and spectators made their way home. They would claim that they were never there. Velma's students were transferred to other classrooms in the area. The Garrett School was never rebuilt. It became a site in a new high-tech treasure hunting—adventure geocaching. Participants used GPS coordinates posted on the Internet to locate a cross-country network of sites. In 2004, items placed in this cache included a 1930 S dime left in memory of Velma Colter.

Lethal violence shattered the serenity of the farmland again. To all appearances, 37-year-old Bill Taylor and his 38-year-old wife, Debbie, were a typical couple struggling to earn a living from their land. They had two children, Doug and Lori.

In the spring of 1994, Debbie visited counselors at Catholic Charities seven times. She spent her time in those sessions wrestling with personal demons, but never once indicated that she had any marital problems. Nonetheless, Bill was certain that the relationship was all she discussed.

He managed to convince himself that his marriage was in serious trouble by the time summer rolled around. His fear gave significance to Debbie's smallest actions. He worried when he observed Debbie standing next to the high school janitor that she stood too close. He worried about the underlying meaning behind Debbie's purchase of the first two-piece bathing suit she had ever owned. His paranoia created a self-fulfilling prophecy.

Anxiety brought out an edgy, argumentative side to Bill. He raged at petty slights. He hurled accusations. When words failed to release his anger, he lashed out with a shove, a slap or a punch.

Although he was tearing apart the very marriage he wanted to preserve, Bill grabbed at opportunities to make things better. He told a friend he was working to win a contest. If he could sell enough bushels of seed corn, he would win the prize of a cruise for two. Bill said he desperately wanted to give his hard-working wife the vacation she deserved but he could not afford to give.

The farmer counted on winning that sail into the sunset to save his failing marriage. When he didn't, Bill pushed Debbie even more. On November 9, he and Debbie had a heated discussion about the possibility of separation. Bill fell asleep that night determined to find a way to avoid divorce at any cost.

He woke in the morning with a plan. Out in the barnyard, he killed one of the cats. He placed its carcass in front of the doorway to the shed housing his combine. He called Debbie over and pointed to the animal as he climbed up into the combine. While Debbie examined the dead body, Bill put the monstrous piece of farm machinery into gear. The massive weight rolled over his wife, crushing the life out of her body. The impact threw Bill from the machine, causing serious injuries to him as well.

The Taylors' son Doug called the Nodaway Sheriff's Department and reported a combine accident. Bill was rushed to the hospital at the Heartland Regional Medical Center in St. Joseph. Debbie was transported to the morgue.

At autopsy, Dr. Michael Berkland determined that Debbie

died from severe internal bleeding and crushing trauma. He also noted that some of the cuts on Debbie's face predated her lethal encounter with the farm equipment. Dr. Berkland's finding raised the specter of past domestic violence.

Sheriff Ben Espey visited Bill in the hospital on Sunday, November 13. He didn't want to go—not for the reason he was there. Espey grew up with Bill and his brother Wayne and considered both men his friends. But duty called and the sheriff set his personal feelings aside.

He read the Miranda Rights out loud to Bill, taking great care not to skip a word or forget any important phrase. When the sheriff finished reading, Bill nodded his head. Espey handed his friend a waiver form. Bill signed it—tossing aside his right to have an attorney present at his questioning.

Espey placed a tape recorder on a table between himself and Bill and said, "I'm gonna record this and it's gonna go to the prosecutor." He pressed the red RECORD button and began his interrogation. Before long Bill confessed that it wasn't an accident—he knew what he was doing when he ran over his wife.

The next day, the Nodaway County prosecutor charged Bill with second-degree murder in the death of Debbie Taylor. Missouri Attorney General Jay Nixon amended the charge in December, raising the bar to first degree. At trial, Bill Taylor was found guilty and sentenced to life behind bars without a chance of parole.

Two acts of violence drew attention to another small town in Nodaway County—Conception, Missouri, originally named Conception Junction. The town of 202 was situated less than twenty miles southeast of Maryville—about thirty miles from Skidmore.

In 1972, Benny Kemper was 15 years old. He didn't have any friends, but he did have a serious crush on Honnie Merrigan. Honnie's brother Billy was in Benny's class. He teased Benny about his infatuation with his sister and belittled his fellow classmate with the typical insensitivity of an adolescent.

On the night of October 10, Benny grabbed a flashlight, a seven-inch knife and a .22-caliber bolt-action rifle from his home. Tonight, he decided he would kill Billy Merrigan.

He crossed an open field near his home and walked a quarter of a mile to Billy's house. When he arrived, no one was home. He crouched down in the darkness to wait for the family's return. Alone with his thoughts, the mind of Benny Kemper turned darker than the night that surrounded him. He reached the conclusion that if he wanted to get away with the murder of Billy, he would have to kill Billy's parents, too.

The Merrigan car pulled into the driveway at 10:40 P.M. Once the family was inside, Benny sliced the phone line and slipped into the basement. He ducked into the shadow of the stairway and listened to the family prepare for bed. The hollow sounds of footsteps on floorboards stopped. The voices above his head stilled. He gave them a little more time to fall asleep. Then, he crept up the steps.

Tension jumped in his stomach. His breath escaped with a stuttering sigh. He made his way to the first-floor bedroom of Billy's parents, Marion and Kathleen Merrigan.

He held the flashlight next to the barrel of his weapon and raised them both. He flipped the switch on the light illuminating Marion's face. He pulled the trigger and shot straight into that face—hitting Marion square in the nose. Pulling the trigger that first time was hard, "but after the first one, it was easy," Benny said.

After killing Marion, he swung his rifle to the right and aimed it at a terrified Kathleen. She could feel the warmth of her husband's spattered blood on her skin. Every other inch of her body felt the chill of fear. Benny shot her twice in the head.

Adrenaline coursed through Benny's body. He wanted to race up the stairs to the second floor, issuing a primal scream as he ascended. He tamped down the urge and took the steps one at a time with uncommon stealth.

Benny eased open the door to Billy's room. Billy was

awake, sitting up in his bed. Before Billy's mind could comprehend the image before his eyes, it was over. Benny shot him three times.

Awakened by the gunfire, Honnie stumbled out of bed and raced down the hall to her brother's room. Benny turned the rifle on her and herded her back to her own room. She begged for her life.

"I won't kill you," he said, "if you take off your clothes."

Honnie forced her fumbling fingers to perform the everyday—but now difficult—task. She stood before him naked. Her body shivered from exposure and intense anxiety. Benny leered at her. Honnie closed her eyes and lowered her head.

Benny turned and stepped toward the door. Honnie grabbed a piece of her discarded clothing and started to put it on. Benny swung around. Startled, Honnie froze. Benny emptied his rifle into her body.

Four dead. Only one member of the family remained. But the oldest daughter, Sue, was out of Benny's reach. Away at college, she was the only family member to survive that night.

The next morning, Benny boarded the bus to go to school. When the driver pulled up in front of the Merrigan home, Benny said, "They won't be coming to school today."

Benny was arrested and tried as an adult. He was sentenced to four 45-year terms—180 years in all. Yet, he was eligible for parole in 1982. His appearances before the parole board since then came often. Kathleen's sister, Marge Wolfer, attended every hearing to argue against his release. Billy insisted he was a changed man. The parole board disagreed. Thirty-three years later, he was still behind bars.

Three decades after Kemper killed four members of the Merrigan family, a lone gunman struck Conception again. On June 9, 2002, 71-year-old Lloyd Jeffress attended the 10:45 A.M. service at the First United Methodist Church in Kearney, Missouri.

The next day, he drove through the peaceful, rolling cornfields of northwest Missouri. High on a knoll sat Conception Abbey, a Benedictine monastery. The centerpiece of the thirty-acre campus was the beautiful Romanesque-style Abbey Church dedicated in 1891.

At 8:35 A.M., Jeffress pulled his green Chevrolet Cavalier into the visitors' parking lot. He stepped out of his car wearing blue work pants and a blue baseball cap. He carried two boxes into the Basilica of the Immaculate Conception. Placing the packages on a table, he opened them with feverish haste. From one he retrieved a MAK-90 assault rifle. The butt of the gun was sawed off—the raw end covered with duct tape. From the other, he pulled out a .22-caliber Ruger.

The armed man walked through a doorway into the monastery. There at the end of the hall, he encountered Brother Damian Larson, meteorologist and groundskeeper of the abbey. Jeffress raised his rifle.

Brother Damian raised his hands. He shouted, "No! No!" Then he crumpled to the floor.

Jeffress walked up to Brother Damian's prone form. He aimed his rifle again and put a bullet through the monk's head.

Abbot Gregory Polan was working in his office when he heard the sound of a gunshot. At first, he thought it was the sound of a window crashing and rushed into the hall to find and assess the damage. Other monks stepped out of their offices and joined him. Then they heard more loud sounds. This time, they recognized the noise as gunfire.

The abbot said, "Go and take cover and lock yourselves in the rooms. I'm going to call 9-1-1."

Back in the hall where Brother Damian's body lay, Reverend Kenneth Reichert and Reverend Norbert Schappler opened the door to their office and poked their heads into the hall. Jeffress shot Reichert in the stomach and then shot Schappler once in the groin and again in the leg. Schappler crawled into the office and called 9-1-1.

Another monk darted into a doorway and shut it behind

him. Jeffress raced after him, but the door was locked and he could not get in.

The gunman headed back to the basilica. He met 85-year-old Reverend Philip Schuster on the way. He shot Schuster twice and pressed on.

Jeffress took a seat in a back pew. He laid down his assault rifle. He put the barrel of the Ruger into his mouth. The thirty-two angels decorating the sacred sanctuary smiled down upon him. Jeffress pulled the trigger and died on the spot.

Two of the wounded monks survived the rampage. But Brother Damian and Reverend Schuster were dead. The abbey grounds crawled with uniforms. Even the United States Bureau of Alcohol, Tobacco and Firearms was called to the scene. They removed a suspicious package the size of a shoe box from the back seat of Jeffress' car.

The ATF agents, with an assist from the Olathe Fire Department, exploded the box. Inside was nothing more than fishing equipment and instructions from a shooting range.

Everyone knew who committed the massacre but no one really knew why. Authorities showed Jeffress' driver's license photo to each individual at the abbey—every monk, every visitor, every lay employee. Not one of them recognized the man.

Relatives suggested that Jeffress was angry with the Catholic Church for the way he was treated after his five-year marriage ended in divorce in 1959. The Church issued annulment papers dissolving the union in 1979.

It was more than twenty years since that final chapter of Jeffress' marriage ended. A search of his apartment uncovered no indication that he was obsessed with the Church or haunted by a long-simmering lust for revenge.

All the authorities had was a loner who at the age of 71 committed suicide after raining carnage down upon a serene refuge in Nodaway County.

As horrific as all these crimes were, the one act in Nodaway County that for decades defined the area to outsiders was the vigilante killing of Ken McElroy. But after the turn of the millennium, a sequence of violent murders inflicted on one generation of the Stinnett family in Skidmore overshadowed the county's entire history of homicide.

15

Born in the late fifties, Becky Harper grew up in Skidmore, swaddled in the arms of small-town America. The turmoil of the 1960s that upended many households only grazed Becky's childhood. Aside from all the traditional holidays, the highlight of every year was the excitement of the annual Punkin Show.

In her senior year of high school—1975–1976—Becky met Cheryl Huston and made a friend for life. When Becky became engaged to Buck Potter, Cheryl helped her pick out the wedding dress, threw her a bridal shower and helped in the planning for the big day. And, of course, Cheryl was Becky's maid of honor.

Becky's twentieth birthday was May 12, 1978. Her wedding day was May 13. For weeks before the ceremony, Cheryl teased that she would kidnap Becky and whisk her away from the wedding.

After the church service in Clearmont, Missouri, Cheryl

got her chance. Outside the sanctuary, Becky realized she'd left behind the clothing she planned to put on at the reception after she took off her wedding dress. Cheryl snatched the clothes, grabbed Becky and off they went.

Cheryl stopped along the way at the A&W convenience store. There, a giddy Becky traipsed through the aisles in her wedding gown. Buck had to drive up Highway 71, across the state line into Iowa and enter the reception hall in Clarinda all alone. He worried that his new wife would be a no-show. After a few laugh-filled detours, Cheryl delivered Becky to the reception.

Buck showed no inclination to follow the community standard of holding a steady job to support his new wife. As a result, that burden fell on Becky. In the fall of 1980, Cheryl got a job at her parents' store, the B&B grocery, where Bo Bowencamp was shot by Ken McElroy earlier that year. The bond between Cheryl and Becky intensified as they worked side by side.

Cheryl thought Becky was the hardest working, most organized and most giving person she had ever met. "There's not a selfish bone in her body," she said.

In late 1979, Becky became pregnant with her first child. Unfortunately, that pregnancy ended in a miscarriage that broke Becky's heart. In early 1981, Becky was pregnant again. The first few months were nerve-wracking as Becky prayed she would not lose this baby and feared that she would miscarry again.

When it looked like she'd carry this child full-term, Becky was jubilant. Cheryl threw her a baby shower to celebrate. Becky's daughter Bobbie Jo was born on December 4, 1981—the same year Ken McElroy died in the streets of Skidmore. She was Becky and Buck's only child.

Bobbie Jo was born with a cleft palate—the fourth most common birth defect in the United States. A cleft palate or cleft lip affected one in every 700 newborns.

It was a congenital problem caused when the opening in the roof of the mouth between the two sides of the palate did not fuse as it should during the development of the fetus. A child born with this condition required a coordinated battery of services including possible surgical procedures, specialized dental care and speech therapy; Bobbie Jo underwent surgery to correct it when she was two years old.

The cleft palate was not the only obstacle to Bobbie Jo learning to speak clearly. Severe ear infections affected her hearing and inflicted excruciating pain on the little girl. When months of medical treatment did not alleviate the problem, Bobbie Jo endured another surgery to put tubes in her ears.

Bobbie Jo was a winsome child just the same. Even her difficulties in speech brought smiles of remembrance decades later to those who knew her when she was small. One of her mispronunciations engraved deep in Cheryl Huston's heart was the recollection of Bobbie Jo saying, "I want to sit in the miggle," when she wanted to squeeze between her mother and Cheryl.

Bobbie Jo was a small child when her father moved down to Texas, leaving his family behind. After a short separation, Becky and Bobbie Jo joined him there. The reunion did not last long. Buck did not provide for his wife and baby, and didn't pay much attention to them either. Becky gave up on the relationship and returned to Skidmore as a single parent.

She needed a paycheck to support herself and her little girl. Unfortunately, employment opportunities in Skidmore were very limited. Cheryl told her mother Lois that she'd give up her own job at the store if her mom would rehire Becky. Lois worked out a plan that enabled her to employ them both.

Becky and Buck's divorce was final in 1985. By the time Bobbie Jo stepped into her teen years, her mother had married again. Bobbie Jo's half-brother Tyler was born when she was 13 years old.

Bobbie Jo was a shy child for most of her life. In the fifth and sixth grades, she was ridiculed a lot because of her

slowness in speech. Many of her school friends still cringe
at the memory of their childhood cruelty to Bobbie Jo.

She underwent a dramatic change, though, when she entered Nodaway-Holt High School in Graham, Missouri. It
was as if she emerged from the cocoon of her introversion,
leaving the obstacles of her childhood behind. She gained a
large measure of popularity and success with ease.

She joined the 4-H club, became a cheerleader, worked
on the school newspaper and yearbook and excelled as an
honor student. She loved riding horses and got tremendous
enjoyment from barrel riding. Bobbie Jo's special rapport
with animals was a great asset for her in this beat-the-clock
sport where communication between horse and rider and the
agility of both outweighed any need for brute strength.

Barrel racing was an event of graceful simplicity—one
woman, three barrels, a horse and a ticking stopwatch. Bobbie Jo—decked out in a long-sleeved shirt, heavy-duty jeans,
sturdy roper boots and a cowboy hat—sat astride a Western
saddle and guided her animal through the course of barrels.

In the traditional configuration, the barrels form a trian-
gle. In Texas style, they were set in a straight line. Riders
streaked their horses as close to these obstacles as possible
to shave seconds off their time. Knocking over a barrel
earned a five-second penalty.

Some young women were drawn to the sport by their
keen sense of competition. Bobbie Jo, though, derived most
of her gratification in the union of herself and the horse—
the two working together to achieve a common goal.

Romance galloped into Bobbie Jo's life, too. She and Zeb
Stinnett grew up in the same neighborhood and knew each
other from childhood. In high school, their casual acquain-
tance grew into a serious relationship. The two were insepa-
rable. Zeb graduated and got a job at the Kawasaki plant.
Kawasaki was a major employer in Nodaway County and its
large facility sat on a hill high above the town of Maryville.

Bobbie Jo graduated in the spring of 2000. Her mother
beamed with pride as Bobbie Jo received her diploma.

Cheryl Huston stood by Becky's side sharing the joy of the moment.

In April 2001, Bobbie Jo got a job at Earl May Feed and Supply just off State Highway 71 and in the shadow of the looming Kawasaki plant. Most of the year, it was a part-time position, but she worked full-time hours during the busy seasons.

She was a dream employee. Her supervisor, Chuck Ellis, said she was dependable and flexible—always willing to fill in when another employee was out sick. She wasn't the kind of worker who needed to have a list prepared for her by her boss. She knew what she had to do and took the initiative to get it done. If she finished her own work, she helped out with other projects and made every minute of her time on the job productive.

Bobbie Jo enjoyed gardening and made the effort to develop a knowledge base on all the store's products. More than for gardening, though, she had an intense love for animals. That passion drew her into the pet corner. She was happiest at work when feeding the small pets—she even liked cleaning the cages and aquariums. Soon, Chuck gave her the responsibility of ordering the fish and small pets—bunnies, guinea pigs, gerbils, rats, mice, finches, doves, cockatiels and parakeets—for the store.

She was quiet, but upbeat—more of a caretaker than a salesperson. She allowed customers to browse unimpeded, but whenever there was a question about one of the critters in her care, she shared her bottomless bounty of knowledge about each one.

She often talked to Chuck and her coworkers about her desire to breed rat terriers. Soon, her dream was a reality named Happy Haven Farms. Her first dog, Tipsy, a 7-year-old white-and-brindle piebald female mini, delivered her first litter on January 17, 2002. From those puppies, Bobbie Jo kept a white-and-red brindle male named Twister. He was an affectionate pup with a passion for chasing squirrels.

Bobbi Jo loved Tipsy—she was her first dog and the

symbol of a dream fulfilled. She heaped praise on her little dog on her website:

> She is so intelligent that she can convey exactly what she's thinking or feeling to you and you know it.

Tipsy's second litter arrived on March 7, 2003. From this group of five, Bobbie Jo kept Belle, a white-and-brindle female who Bobbie Jo wrote was "a true athlete"—able to jump five feet straight up from a standing position. Belle was a natural for agility competition.

Bobbie Jo had a dog-lover's philosophy in breeding:

> Our dogs are bred as house pets first and foremost as we live, sleep, and play with our dogs . . .

She also knew that it was a serious business:

> they are bred to excel as well in hunting, conformation (UKC or NKC reg'd pups only), as well as performance events (weight pull, agility, obedience). Our litters are planned up to 2 years in advance and the potential parents are picked over to maximize their good qualities, as well as vet checked prior to each breeding. We offer our puppies to GREAT homes only.

She was quite particular about who adopted her puppies. Each prospective owner filled out an application. The two-page form requested details about the number and ages of the people in the household, whether the home was rented or owned and how much time each day would be devoted to their new pet. She also wanted to know if the applicant had ever euthanized an animal and why, and whether or not puppy obedience classes were planned.

In no time, Bobbie Jo earned the respect and friendship of many in the rat terrier community. Quite a few other breeders contacted her for advice on a regular basis. Her forte was the genetic factors involved with the breed—her interest in this area was fueled by her awareness of the congenital aspect of her own birth defect. Her emails were full of technical language and the percentages of lineage overlap. Many swore by her recommendations for good breeding pairs. She was an acknowledged expert on the genetics of the breed—but Bobbie Jo never presented herself as the final word on rat terrier breeding. A common phrase in her messages offering advice was "as I learn more." She was modest about her expertise, but others found her remarkable. They felt she knew as much as a studious breeder with decades of experience.

The hereditary factors determining coat color in puppies was of particular interest to Bobbie Jo. She was determined to produce a reliable line of brindle-colored rat terriers even though that coloration was not recognized by some of the registries. In fact, it was considered a disqualifying flaw by some. Bobbie Jo loved that coloration, though, and her goal was to change the perception and gain acceptance of it. She had a focus in her mission that went well beyond her years.

A fellow rat terrier fancier in North Carolina, Dyanne Siktar, had a similar interest, but she focused on the pearl coat color. The two exchanged many emails and talked on the telephone about their enthusiasms. Having never met face-to-face, Dyanne developed her own mental portrait of Bobbie Jo. Because of the wealth of knowledge she possessed and her soothing and mature-sounding voice, Dyanne assumed she was in her fifties. She was quite surprised later when she learned how young her fellow breeder really was.

In April 2003, Bobbie Jo resigned from her job at Earl May to accept a higher-paying position at the Kawasaki plant. She married her childhood sweetheart, Zeb Stinnett, on April 26, 2003, in the old stone sanctuary of Skidmore Christian Church.

The original congregation met in a building dedicated in January 1895. A newer building erected on the same site in

1928 was where the couple exchanged their vows. Reverend
Harold Hamon officiated over the service. Betty Nelson
baked and decorated the wedding cake and played the piano
for the ceremony. A beaming Bobbie Jo—dressed in white—
clutched her grandfather's arm as he walked her down the
aisle.

The newlyweds rented a small bungalow on Elm Street—
just a couple of blocks from Newton's corner. All the money
Bobbie Jo made from her rat terrier business was stashed
away as the couple worked to fulfill their dream of buying
their own home.

Zeb's step-grandmother, Jo Ann Stinnett, remembered
Bobbie Jo as a sweet and considerate young woman. Zeb
drove a new blue Mustang with a big booming, bass sound.
He loved to ride down country roads feeling the beat of the
music vibrate in the steering wheel beneath his hands. When
they pulled into the driveway of Zeb's grandparents' home,
Bobbie Jo always made him turn it down. She knew the
amped-up sound would disturb Zeb's ailing grandfather Babe.

Bobbie Jo became a regular in the dog show circuit and was
a natural in the ring. She handled the dogs with a gentle patience that produced top-notch behavior and performance
from every dog she showed. She was a rat terrier breed in-
spector and licensed judge for the National Kennel Club,
and press secretary for a United Kennel Club.

Sometimes when she traveled to the exhibitions, she
shared a hotel room with Tracey Ramirez, a Leavenworth,
Kansas, breeder she met online. Other times, Zeb accompanied her to the shows. He wasn't involved in the breeding effort, but encouraged his wife's passionate interest.

On April 3, 2004, a couple of weeks before a dog show in
Abilene, Kansas, Lisa Montgomery wrote to Bobbie Jo
Stinnett.

> It has been a busy week here. With 5 active pups, 3 of
> which my daughter is working with on crate training, litter

box training and stacking on her table, her room is more like our kennel room here! The kids are talking about switching bedrooms to give Kayla and the pups their own room even if it means someone else has to share a bedroom.

We are still planning on making the Abilene, Kansas show on the 17th with at least two of the pups depending on how well training goes. Kayla is excited about this as this will be her first show.

Bobbie Jo responded:

Lisa,
I will be at the show. Cannot wait to meet you. We will be bringing Diamond down for the Standard Variety puppy class.

At the show later that month, Bobbie Jo was pregnant. And Lisa Montgomery—clad in maternity clothes—told everyone she was carrying twins.

16

In the months after the show, Lisa and Bobbie Jo stayed in contact online. They chatted about puppies and breeding plans. They compared notes about the progress of their pregnancies and shared dreams about their babies' futures.

Another woman in the rat terrier chat group announced in April that she was pregnant with twins. Lisa Montgomery contacted her via instant messenger and wrote, "I've got you beat!" She added that her twins were due to arrive first—on December 12.

A few days later, Lisa contacted the woman again. She said that she was knitting a blanket for the woman's babies. The mother-to-be thought it was a little odd—but nice—that someone she only knew online would go to that much trouble for her.

In June, the woman miscarried her twins when the fetuses were just fourteen weeks old. She never heard from Lisa Montgomery again.

* * *

That spring, Bobbie Jo fell in love with Fonzi, a puppy she
spotted online. He was a white-and-blue-fawn blanket-back
male born on February 29, 2004, at Calico Run Kennels in
Austin, Texas. Bobbie Jo contacted kennel owner Pat Kennedy to discuss the possibility of joint ownership of Fonzi.

After several exchanges of emails and telephone calls,
Pat agreed. She made arrangements to meet Bobbie Jo at the
dog show in Norman, Oklahoma, on May 16, and turn Fonzi
over to Bobbie Jo's care.

Pat checked into her hotel room and then went up one
floor to where Bobbie Jo was staying. When she entered, she
saw a rat terrier lying on her back sound asleep with her feet
stuck up straight in the air. Bobbie Jo had the dog's back
paws in her hands, filing down her little nails. Pat had seen a
lot of squirming and a lot of reluctant acquiescence from
dogs whose nails were being trimmed and filed, but never
before had she seen one fall asleep in the process.

Bobbie Jo continued to amaze Pat throughout the show.
She had a way with animals that created an instant and unbelievable bond. Every dog Bobbie Jo encountered melted
in her presence and seemed to have no greater desire in life
than to be close to her. Rat terriers were a passion for her and
somehow the dogs knew it and loved her for it.

2004 was a big year for Bobbie Jo's business. Tipsy had
her third and final litter in September—she retired from
breeding after that. Bobbie Jo also bred Belle, one of Tipsy's
second litter, to Jason Dawson's male, Mighty Samson. That
litter was in high demand. She barely had time to announce
it online before she had a waiting list for five of the pups.
She also bred Diamond, a black, tan and white female she
got from the Duke family in St. Charles, Missouri. She
planned a second litter for Diamond in 2005. The sire for
that litter would be her new co-owned addition, Fonzi.

Bobbie Jo was delighted with the success of her rat terrier
breeding, but it was nothing to compare to her excitement

over the child she had on the way. Her due date was January
19, and she was ecstatic.

She and Zeb batted around possible baby names as soon as
they knew a baby was on the way. They decided on Zebadiah
if the baby was a boy, Victoria Jo if it was a girl. By early November, they knew Bobbie Jo was carrying their daughter. As
soon as Bobbie Jo knew her baby would be a girl, she regis-
tered at Wal-Mart. Her list included newborn onesies, pink
and yellow blankets, pink burp cloths and a diaper bag.

Bobbie Jo talked often to Pat Kennedy about her hopes
and dreams for her baby girl. She already planned to take
Victoria Jo with her to dog shows right away. She wanted her
to grow up comfortable with the venue. She couldn't wait to
teach her how to care for the dogs, how to show them and the
basics and importance of genetics in dog breeding. She envisioned Victoria Jo growing into her future partner and friend.

In early October, Lisa Montgomery posted at an online rat
terrier site:

> I lost one of the twins. It's so terrible, but they
> saved one twin.

On another site, she griped about her child support from
Carl Boman. She complained that her attorney also represented Kevin's ex-wife. Kevin was hauled into court nearly
every year for an increase in child support, and the difference was garnished from his wages within two weeks. For
some reason Lisa did not understand, that same attorney was
only able to get Carl into court on one occasion, and that one
time, she said, delays ran on for months.

Later that month, Kevin Montgomery told Reverend
Wheatley that he'd felt the baby kick inside of his wife's
body. When Wheatley saw Lisa he said, "You look too thin
to be eight months pregnant."

"I always have small babies," she said.

* * *

The rat terrier enthusiasts were surprised and delighted when the very pregnant Bobbie Jo Stinnett showed up at a dog show in mid-November. Bobbie Jo felt uncomfortable in her awkward body. She changed outfits at least five times in an attempt to find something to wear that didn't bind.

Despite her discomfort, Bobbie Jo did well at the show. Diamond won one Reserve—second place—ribbon, Best Female in two categories and two Best of Winners ribbons. Fonzi earned Best Male in three different categories and in the final multiple breed competition, he was awarded a Best of Winners ribbon.

It was Fonzi's first show and his success blew Bobbie Jo away. Each ribbon prompted a call to Pat Kennedy. "I hardly worked with him at all," she said. "I just brought him along to get familiar with the ring."

Bobbie Jo's excitement was boundless, she even broke into tears of joy on a couple of the calls. Fonzi's first show brought him within three points of earning his championship. Bobbie Jo and Pat made plans to go together with Fonzi to a dog show in January to let him win the final points he needed.

Bobbie Jo promised to teach Pat everything she knew about the breed and the genetics of breeding. Pat was delighted. She could not think of anyone else who would be a more knowledgeable—and giving—teacher.

That same month, Bobbie Jo's friends gathered together to throw a baby shower for the radiant young mother-to-be. It was a joyous occasion—a celebration of life and the arrival of a new generation.

It was also the month that Lisa Montgomery purchased a home birth kit. It was the type that midwives often used to deliver babies at home. On the Internet, Lisa visited MapQuest on multiple occasions and downloaded directions from her house in Melvern to the home of Bobbie Jo Stinnett in Skidmore.

She sat engrossed at her desk for a prolonged period of

time on November 17. Her attention was riveted by an on-line video of a doctor performing a cesarean section.

Lisa quit her job at Wendy's on Interstate Highway 35 before Thanksgiving. She told her employer that she needed to cut back on her workload because her baby was due in December. Desiree and Chelsea worked at that Wendy's, too. They picked up some of the slack caused by their co-worker's absence—logging more hours than usual up until mid-December.

In early December, Bobbie Jo paid a visit to her former em-ployer, Earl May Feed and Supply. She often stopped by the shop with fish she bred in her tanks and traded them in for other fish the shop had in stock.

This time, she wanted to buy a few new fish for her tank. While she was there, she chatted with Chuck Ellis and her former coworkers. Bobbie Jo appeared even more animated and happy than usual.

Isabel Phelon, the Montgomerys' landlady, drove past her ten-ants' home and stopped when she saw Kevin outside. When she asked him how his wife was doing, Kevin said, "Lisa's still working, but she is expecting her baby next week."

On December 10, Lisa Montgomery wrote on the rat ter-rier boards about her difficulty in obtaining good photos of her dogs:

> Right now it is worse—I can not get down on the floor to take better pictures due to being pregnant and getting back up is a story in itself.

She wrote that she thought about putting Angel—the rat terrier she wanted to photograph—standing up on a table, but

> Angel does not like heights, and I didn't think now was the time to introduce her for the sake of a few pictures—lol. But I tried!

She added that her due date was December 16.

That same day in Osage County District Court, Lisa's first husband, Carl Boman, filed for custody of two of the four children born during his marriage to Lisa. The oldest child, Desiree, would soon be 18 years old and could decide on her own. The youngest, 14-year-old Kayla, wanted to stay in Georgia with the family who currently cared for her. But the two middle children, C.J. and Chelsea, ages 15 and 16, expressed a desire to live with their dad, citing difficulties with their mother.

As a part of his case, Carl planned to question Lisa's mental state by saying she faked pregnancies. Lisa would either have to admit that she was not pregnant or Carl could prove it, enhancing his probability of gaining custody.

That same night was parents' and seniors' night at the Marais Des Cygnes Valley High School basketball game in Melvern. Although Lisa wore maternity clothes, the people who saw her that night found it hard to believe that she was due in less than a week's time.

After the game, Lisa went online and posted a message next to her Internet name:

Baby any day, maybe today.

17

On December 15, Jason Dawson logged on to MSN Messenger. From her home computer, Lisa Montgomery joined him online. If he had known he was chatting with Lisa, he would have found a quick, polite way to sign off and return later when she was not there.

Jason, however, had no clue to the real identity of the person he engaged in e-conversation. He thought he was talking to Darlene Fischer, a woman who was eager to get a rat terrier puppy for her children for Christmas.

She told him that she couldn't take the puppy home right away because she was going on vacation. She wanted to put a deposit down, though, before she left town. Jason thought Darlene was a nice person. He appreciated her excitement about surprising her children. He was a parent, too.

Jason wanted to help her in her puppy quest and asked her where she lived. Darlene told him she was in Fairfax, Missouri. Jason knew that town was just a half hour's drive from

Skidmore and thought of Bobbie Jo Stinnett right away. He
knew Bobbie Jo had puppies for sale. He gave Bobbie Jo's
email address to Darlene. He thought he was doing Bobbie
Jo a favor.

At 4:22 P.M., Lisa Montgomery—using her Darlene Fischer alias—sent a note via instant messenger to Bobbie Jo
Stinnett:

> I was recommended to you by Jason Dawson and
> have been unable to reach you by either phone or
> email. Please get in touch with me soon as we are
> considering the purchase of one of your puppies . . .

For twenty minutes, Bobbie Jo and Darlene chattered in
instant messenger. They made plans to meet at Bobbie Jo's
home the next day.

Early in the afternoon of December 16, Deann Hensley of
Bedford, Iowa, was shopping at the Wal-Mart in Maryville,
Missouri—just a half hour's drive from Skidmore. She strolled
through the aisles with her mother and her 6-month-old baby.
Her baby started to cry while she was browsing through CDs
in the music department.

Lisa Montgomery approached her with a smile. "What a
beautiful baby," she said.

Deann thanked her for the compliment, then turned back
to her child to soothe her and wipe away her tears.

Lisa continued to hover nearby. "I'll hold your baby while
you look around if she's not scared of me," she offered.

Unease rumbled through Deann. She held her baby
tighter. She looked at the stranger who wanted to lay hands
on her child. Behind Lisa's smile she saw unhealthy hunger.
In that hunger, she saw danger. She told herself that this sudden onset of paranoid suspicion was just her maternal in-
stinct run amok. But still she did not want that woman near

her baby. She smiled a tight, polite smile, nodded in farewell and walked away from Lisa Montgomery. She moved as quickly as decorum would allow, putting as much distance as possible between her baby and the needy, dirty-blond stranger. She breathed easier when Lisa Montgomery was out of sight.

Lisa watched the mother and child leave until they disappeared into another aisle. Then she drifted over to the baby department to browse. The Wal-Mart security cameras followed her every move. They captured images of everything she did that day in the store, but they were blind to the motivations behind her actions. Lisa selected a few items of baby clothing, paid for her purchase and left the store.

She turned left out of the parking lot, driving the compact red car, laden with a burden of dust and mud picked up on the dirt roads of Melvern. At the last light before leaving Maryville, she turned right onto the road to Skidmore.

She followed the byway up and down hills. Around gentle curves and major bends. Through fallow fields barren in the cold.

She entered Skidmore. She drove past the brick Skidmore Museum. Past the block where emptiness prevailed and only the bar beckoned. At the intersection, the highway turned left. Lisa drove straight ahead—down Elm Street to the white bungalow of Zeb and Bobbie Jo Stinnett.

Bobbie Joe was at home on Elm Street awaiting the arrival of Darlene Fischer. She was excited about the visit. She loved the opportunity to show off her puppies.

At 2:30, her telephone rang. It was her mother, Becky Harper, calling to ask if Bobbie Jo could pick her up from work at Sumy Oil—just a couple of blocks away. If Becky had looked out the window at that time, she would have seen Lisa Montgomery's dirty red car drive past Sumy Oil.

Bobbie Jo explained to her mother that she couldn't leave

the house just yet—she was expecting someone to look at
the dogs. As the two women chatted, Bobbie Jo heard a
knock on her door. She looked out the front window and saw
a red Toyota parked in front of her house.

"Oh, they're here," she said to her mother. "I've got to go."

18

When Bobbie Jo answered her front door, Lisa Montgomery stood on her front porch. Did Bobbie Jo recognize the woman she'd met at dog shows? Or did she just think "Darlene Fischer" looked familiar?

Whatever questions raced through Bobbie Jo's mind, either they did not create any anxiety, or Lisa—the smooth-talking, experienced liar—allayed her fears with ease. If recognized as Lisa Montgomery, Lisa could have claimed that she was just in the neighborhood and wanted to see Bobbie Jo's litter of pups. Otherwise, it was as the oddly familiar Darlene Fischer that Lisa entered the Stinnett home.

There was no physical evidence to indicate that Lisa Montgomery used any force to obtain entry. There were no forensic indications that anything untoward happened in any of the rooms the two women passed to reach the converted bedroom that housed the litter of rat terriers.

In that room, where the puppies squirmed and yipped in celebration of new life, Bobbie Jo Stinnett was comfortable enough with her visitor to turn her back on her. Lisa seized that opportunity. She threw a rope around Bobbie Jo's neck and jerked it tight.

Bobbie Jo experienced a moment of mental numbness from the shock of the ugly surprise. Her biological imperative for survival, however, reacted instantly. She bucked in defiance, driving Lisa backward. Bobbie Jo's feet kicked at her attacker—some thrusts hitting their mark, others connecting with nothing but empty air. Bobbie Jo struggled to catch a breath. She clawed at the rope around her throat.

Lisa's jaw tightened in determination. Her hands shook as she pulled on the rope with all of her strength. She held her death grip until Bobbie Jo's thrashing body quieted. She did not let up until Bobbie Jo slumped over, supported only by the binding around her neck. Then, Lisa eased her hold on the rope and Bobbie Jo slid unconscious to the floor.

Lisa rushed into the kitchen. She flexed the cramps out of her hands as she ran. She grabbed a three-inch paring knife. She knelt on the floor by Bobbie Jo. She knew every second counted. There was no time to spare—the baby's life was at stake.

She sunk the knife in at the top of Bobbie Jo's distended belly. She sliced downward with care and patience. She saw the blood sketch a bright red line in the trail of the knife. She saw it pool and slide down Bobbie Jo's sides.

Bobbie Jo was not dead yet. She twitched. The pain of the incision revived her. She cried out. She sat up and threw off her attacker. She knocked away the knife. She staggered to her feet and lunged for the knife, but Lisa held on to it. The struggle, though, left cuts all over both of her hands.

Lisa grabbed the rope and tried to get it around Bobbie Jo's throat. Bobbie Jo tried to escape from her tormentor. She fought for her life—and for the life of the baby she loved sight unseen.

Blood continued to flow from the gaping lateral slice in
Bobbie Jo's body. It pooled on the floor. The soles of Bobbie
Jo's feet fought to maintain their purchase on the slick, red
boards. Clots formed at the site of the wound and dropped
with a splat on the smeared blood on the floor.

Lisa secured the rope and tightened it around Bobbie Jo's
neck again. Bobbie Jo reached behind with both hands. She
grabbed and yanked Lisa's hair as hard as she could. She
pulled strands out by the roots. That was not enough to stop
Lisa Montgomery.

Lisa squeezed tighter—her strength and determination
fueled by a sociopathic desperation. When Bobbie Jo's body
went limp once again, Lisa still held on. This time, she
would be sure Bobbie Jo was dead. She throttled her victim
for a full five minutes, then eased the dead weight to the
floor—she did not want to harm the baby. Bobbie Jo lay
dead; in her hands, she clenched clumps of dirty blonde hair.

Lisa kneeled down again at Bobbie Jo's side to continue
her grisly work. She finished cutting through the layers of the
skin. She sliced again, this time through the layer of fat cells.
Then a third laceration parted the layer of muscle. When the
cut was long enough and deep enough, Lisa saw the prize she
sought—Bobbie Jo's uterus. She sliced the womb open with
a care that indicated knowledge or experience.

Lisa reached into Bobbie Jo's bloody, desecrated body and
pulled out a wriggling baby girl. She sliced the umbilical cord
in two. She tied off the end of the cord connected to the child.
Wrapping the baby in a blanket, she held her tight in her arms,
breathing deeply—inhaling the scent of the child she now
claimed as her own. It was as if a demented magic spell had
taken hold of her. As is typical of infant abductors, the moment that little body was next to hers, a fantastical delusion
seized her. It said: This is my baby. I saved my baby from that
woman. If I had not taken her, she surely would have died.

Lisa grabbed the knife and raced to her car. She drove out
of Skidmore heading straight to Maryville. She took the highway and continued south down to St. Joseph. Around Kansas

City. Across the Missouri–Kansas state line. Westward to
Topeka. She pulled into Long John Silver's and parked in
their lot.

Somewhere between Skidmore and the fast food restaurant, she cleaned up herself and her baby. The violent assault
on Bobbie Jo left smears of blood on her clothing and her
arms. She looked normal now. A mother and her infant.
Haggard but happy after a successful birth. She called her
husband, Kevin, and told him the good news.

19

Lisa Montgomery was raised at a time when women made great strides in government, corporations and every other walk in life. Despite these advances, Lisa remained mired in the antiquated notion that a woman's value was based solely on her ability to reproduce and nurture.

This pathetic self-image led Lisa to a crisis point, where she made the decision to cross a line that was beyond normal contemplation. She transitioned from an emotionally disturbed woman to a heartless murderer with frightening ease.

The path she followed to become a killer began while she was still in her teens. Her frenzied procreation with her first husband—four babies in less than four years—was a shadowy premonition of what was to come. She was a bright young woman who sensed the stress fractures in her relationship from the start. In response, she stayed pregnant because she thought it was the only way to stay married.

After the fourth child, however, her husband, Carl, did not want any more mouths to feed. He insisted on a tubal ligation. Without that procedure, Lisa might have become a one-woman population explosion.

When Carl left Lisa and moved to Arkansas, Lisa had no sense of identity—she needed a man for that. She fought for her relationship in the only way she knew: another pregnancy. Carl fell for her ruse the first time. He remarried Lisa—but, of course, she did not produce a child.

When Lisa's idyllic illusion of a good marriage started to crumble again, she announced yet another pregnancy. This time, Carl didn't fall for it. But he did stay with her and even agreed to move the family out of state when Lisa's embarrassment over the faked conception became more than she could bear.

In New Mexico with a husband immune to the pregnancy ploy, Lisa was deprived of the only weapon she thought she had to maintain the relationship. When the marriage ended, that failure reinforced Lisa's conviction that she was worthless without her ability to bear a child for her man.

She moved to Kansas, met Kevin Montgomery, and in no time was plotting to marry him. She thought that if Kevin believed she were pregnant, he'd follow her to the altar. She was surprised when, instead, he gave her the money for an abortion. Still, she didn't give up on her dream of matrimony. She played on Kevin's sympathy by creating a new pregnancy in her teenage years—one where her family deceived her and stole her baby away.

After that heart-breaking tale, Kevin was hooked—one more faked pregnancy and Lisa was Mrs. Kevin Montgomery. After exchanging vows, she claimed that pregnancy, too, ended in miscarriage. When the marriage to Kevin showed signs of distress, she played the game once again.

It seemed mind-boggling that Lisa was able to fool so many people so much of the time. She pulled it off because

Bobbie Jo
with a sleeping
rat terrier pup.
*Photo courtesy
Pat Kennedy.*

Bobbie Jo at her
first Christmas.
Photo courtesy Becky Harper.

Becky Potter proudly
poses with her six-month-old
daughter, Bobbie Jo.
Photo courtesy Becky Harper.

Summer 1983—Bobbie Jo in
wading pool with friends
Jody and Jaimie.
Photo courtesy Becky Harper.

Bobbie Jo in April 2001.
*Photo courtesy
Becky Harper.*

Bobbie Jo practicing barrel-racing.
Photo courtesy Becky Harper.

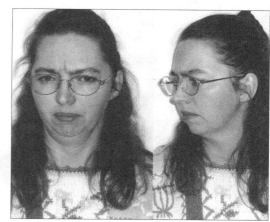

Lisa
Montgomery's
mug shot.
*Photo courtesy
Nodaway County
Sheriff's
Department.*

The Melvern, Kansas, water tower from the center of town.
Photo by Diane Fanning.

Kevin and Lisa Montgomery's home.
Photo by Diane Fanning.

The Whistle Stop Café, where Lisa and Kevin
showed off their new baby. *Photo by Diane Fanning.*

Skidmore Public
Library.
*Photo by Diane
Fanning.*

Newton's Corner in Skidmore.
Photo by Diane Fanning.

Bobbie Jo & Jeb's home
on Elm Street.
Photo by Diane Fanning.

White House award ceremony in the Oval Office: (*l to r*) Corporal
Jeffrey Owen, Missouri State Highway Patrol; Sergeant David Merrill,
Missouri State Highway patrol; Sheriff Ben Espey, Nodaway County
Sheriff's Department; President George W. Bush; Special Agent Kurt
Lipanovich, FBI; Investigator Randy Strong, Maryville Department of
Public Safety. *Photo courtesy Ben Espey.*

Items seized from Lisa Montgomery's car including the knife used to perform the cesarean section and a photo of a litter of newborn rat terrier pups. *Photo courtesy Nodaway County Sheriff's Department.*

Lisa's dirty red Toyota.
Photo courtesy Nodaway County Sheriff's Department.

Bobbie Jo's headstone. *Photo by Diane Fanning.*

STINNETT
BOBBIE JO POTTER
DEC. 4, 1981
DEC. 16, 2004
BELOVED WIFE AND MOTHER OF VICTORIA

she had more in her arsenal than a canny gift for falsehood. She also had physical symptoms like the hardened abdomen she displayed to her sister.

There were two possible reasons for Lisa's physical symptoms. One was pseudocyesis, a form of psychosis causing a woman to seek attention by faking or lying about a pregnancy. Many of these women learned how to swallow air to bloat their abdomens.

Another possibility was that Lisa was in the midst of a disassociative episode where she genuinely believed she was pregnant. Women in this condition experienced a myriad of pregnancy symptoms including a distended belly, enlarged breasts and the absence of menses. When forced to face the truth, these women often spiraled down into a deep depression.

Dr. Jack Gorman, chief of psychiatry at the Mt. Sinai Medical Center and professor of neuroscience at the Mt. Sinai School of Medicine told a *New York Times* reporter, "In these cases, a woman might have a delusion that 'That's my baby in that woman, she's stolen it, and if I don't rescue it, she's going to kill it,' and the motivation is just so overwhelming that you just lose contact with reality. It's hard for people who've never had this experience to understand, but the voices and hallucinations and demands become overwhelming."

At the same time as she played at pregnancy, she also worked to achieve custody of Teddy's son. When that plot fell apart, she tried to extort money from her ex-husband to buy a baby. From her point of view, he pressured her into a tubal ligation and now he would pay. Carl, however, did not have the money she needed even if he'd been willing to give it to her.

Lisa, though, was still determined to get what she wanted. She met a woman online who was pregnant with twins. Now Lisa claimed to be pregnant with twins. She tried to build a relationship with her by sharing pregnancy experiences and sending a handmade gift.

When that woman lost her twins, Lisa purported to have lost one of hers. She set her sights on another woman—Bobbie Jo Stinnett. Bobbie Jo was expecting a single child. Now, Lisa ostensibly carried one baby, too.

20

Somehow, Lisa Montgomery thought she could get away with her charade. She was content in her deceptive fantasy—but law enforcement was not.

The investigation gathered strength with every passing moment. Local, state and federal officials worked in unison to shatter the illusions of a woman whose identity was still unknown.

While computer forensic specialists tracked down Darlene Fischer, the FBI sent agents to question the third person in the online discussion, Jason Dawson of Rat Time Kennels in Kansas City, Missouri. He told them, "I don't think that Darlene Fischer had anything to do with this—she just wanted to look at puppies."

In the coming hours, those words reverberated in Jason's head. He was sickened by the truth and felt more stupid and foolish than he ever had in his life. This betrayal of his trust

destroyed any belief he had in the decency of his fellow
man, and marked him for life.

With the secrets of Bobbie Jo's computer revealed, law enforcement rolled into Kansas south of Topeka. They stopped
at the white farmhouse. The home looked so innocent—so
all-American. The original dwelling featured a deep porch
running across the length of the front. It was topped by a
graceful gabled roof. Attached to one side was a plain, two-
story addition built with practicality—not aesthetics—in
mind.

Investigators closed in on this modest home with a torrent
of questions. Lisa denied any wrongdoing at first. But the
questions did not cease. They pounded down with greater in-
tensity until the dam burst and Lisa spewed out the awful
truth.

At 2:30, the Amber Alert was lifted. At that same time,
the telephone rang at the Siktar home. Special Agent Kurt
Lipanovich said, "Dyanne, you are a hero."

"Did you find the baby?" she asked.

"Yes."

"Is she okay?"

"Yes, she's fine. But there's so much going on here, I
can't talk right now."

A little after 3, Sheriff Espey stepped outside to face a battery of forty or fifty microphones and news cameras. He knew
this case was important to him, to his county and to the people
of Skidmore, but he was amazed at the national spotlight—
Larry King even called him at home.

He approached the bank of microphones and a hush spread
through the gathered media horde. "We're going to be really
brief. Is everybody ready? This conference won't last long.
We've been into this investigation for twenty-three and a half
hours and we have some really good breaking news. They
have located a baby girl. We're waiting testing—medical
testing—to see if it's going to be our child that's missing. We
feel really good about it. I think with the highway patrol and

the FBI here, there was a lot of manpower put into this, a lot of hard investigative work. Right now, there are investigators doing questioning."

Excitement and elation rippled through the crowd. To Espey, it seemed the reporters were reacting to more than a development in a great story. The media before him appeared overjoyed at the news on a more personal level.

"What we can tell you is—this baby crossed state lines into Kansas. We're not going to give you any locations on that, because we really don't want press charging that angle," Espey continued. "There's still investigation that needs to be done on this."

In response to a question about the baby, Espey said, "The child appears to be healthy and in good shape. The child is at a hospital right now, being checked out by a pediatrician and we have no indications that the child was hurt in any way. And the child is probably going to be okay. That's the information we are getting."

A voice shouted out, "You're not ready to confirm anything?"

"We're not going to confirm this one hundred percent. But, it's about as good as it can get."

Isabel Phelon spent the morning in Lyndon getting her hair done. When she drove past the home she rented to Lisa and Kevin in Melvern, she didn't notice anything out of the ordinary. That afternoon, she went down to the well to check on the water pump. From there she had a clear view of the Montgomery home. Cars marked with law enforcement logos as well as unmarked—but official-looking—vehicles crowded in the yard and out on the street. Her first thought was: I wonder if Lisa lost her baby?

She hopped in her car, and traveled past the house at regular speed, but didn't see anyone she knew in the yard, and couldn't figure out what was happening. She turned around a little ways up the street and drove past the Montgomery home again—this time she crawled down the road.

Her slow speed caught the attention of officers, who approached her car. "What's going on?" she asked them. "I am the landlord."

"This is a crime scene," they told her before asking her to move on. They were clearly not in the mood to talk in more detail, so Isabel drove home with more questions in her mind than she had when she left the house a few moments before.

At 3:30, the five-pound, eleven-ounce infant entered the Stormont-Vail Regional Health Care Center emergency room in Topeka. Personnel transferred her at once to the neonatal intensive care unit. Doctors reported that she was responding normally for a baby born one month premature.

Blood was drawn for DNA testing. They all believed this was the baby of Bobbie Jo Stinnett, but they wanted proof.

After a couple of hours of questioning, Lisa Montgomery was arrested and taken to the Wynadotte County Jail in Kansas City, Kansas. A stunned Kevin Montgomery was not charged with a crime. He was brought in, however, for intensive interrogation.

Authorities performed a search of Lisa Montgomery. They photographed the cuts on her hands. They scraped underneath her fingernails. Tests of that material showed that it was a genetic commingling of the DNA of Bobbie Jo Stinnett and Lisa Montgomery.

With the residents removed from their home on South Adams Road, a search of the house and vehicles began in earnest. Hundreds of documents, papers, receipts and other items were seized. In the end, most of these articles proved to have no evidentiary value, but investigators exercised abundant caution to ensure that nothing was overlooked.

Amid the pile of irrelevant material, the forensic technicians found a treasure trove of items of significant forensic importance. From the trunk of Lisa's car, they removed a rope—covered with blood and hair. Genetic testing revealed the DNA of Bobbie Jo Stinnett. A kitchen knife that Lisa identified as the one she used to cut open her victim held more evidence. They tested the blood on the blade of the knife. It was a mixture of the DNA of Bobbie Jo and Victoria Jo. On the handle, analysis revealed a blend of the genetic material of three individuals: the baby, the mother and Lisa Montgomery.

At 4 P.M., Lisa's mother Judy received a phone call from her niece in Texas. "Is it true Lisa has a baby?" she asked.

"Yes," Judy said.

"Is it a girl?"

"Yes," Judy said and then listened with dread as her niece shared what she knew about the tragic story of Bobbie Jo Stinnett and her baby girl.

21

Judy Shaughnessy was hungry for more details. She wanted information that would erase her suspicions about her daughter Lisa and ease her heart. She didn't want to run into town to pick up a newspaper. She'd be sure to run into someone she knew and that was the last thing she wanted right now. She also wanted news that was fresher than that morning's headlines. She didn't have cable TV and she didn't use a computer.

She called her daughter Jerri and shared her fears. "Would you get online and find everything you can find about the murder in Skidmore and read it to me?"

Jerri had no problem locating articles: the Internet—like the media—was drowning in coverage. Jerri opened one story after another and read them on the phone to her mother. With each word, Judy's horror escalated. The more she heard, the more the possibility that Lisa was responsible for Bobbie Jo's death grew. By the time Jerri finished reading, it was an undeniable probability. Judy had known miserable times over the years, but today was shaping into the worst day of her life.

Jerri and her sister Patty dropped everything and rushed to be by their mother's side at her farm in Lyndon. Outside, nothing ruffled the feathers of the geese or the chickens. Placid cows chewed their cud. The pigs snuffled about and the goats grazed. All were oblivious to the turmoil brewing inside the home. The family sat in front of Judy's television. Their collective dread sucked the air out of the room and the hope out of their hearts as they watched the news reports of Lisa's arrest. They could doubt the reality of Lisa's culpability no longer.

They had known Lisa was deceptive and manipulative. They thought she was capable of doing or saying almost anything to get what she wanted. But this? This was too much. They never once imagined she was willing to kill for what she wanted. They never suspected she would go this far.

About ten minutes before the evening news came on the air, Melvern resident Darrell Schultze called Reverend Mike Wheatley. "Are you in the middle of all of this?"

"In the middle of what?" the minister asked.

As Darrell explained the breaking news about Lisa's arrest and Bobbie Jo's death, Wheatley's spirits sagged. The baby he cradled in his arms that morning was stolen from another woman? Her mother was murdered? And the person responsible stood right here in his home? Just steps away from his church? A member of his own congregation? It was overwhelming and it made no sense. But then, the visit from Kevin and Lisa that morning didn't make a lot of sense either. The questions he and his wife tossed around after the Montgomerys left now had clear but dreadful answers.

The news spread over Melvern faster than locust through a field of wheat. Whether they knew Lisa Montgomery or not, the shock was intense. Interest in the story was not confined to southeast Kansas and northwest Missouri. It flooded living rooms with horror from coast-to-coast. Many had never heard of such a crime.

After the homicide of Laci Peterson and others, the public will understood the vulnerability of a pregnant woman to an act of violence committed by spouse or boyfriend. Now they were awakened to a new macabre twist.

Although rare, kidnapping by caesarean section was common enough to merit serious study by forensic specialists. Between 1983 and 2000, there were 199 reported cases of infant abduction—thirty of these involved acts of violence. Six of these violent kidnappings involved the caesarean section, according to an article published in the *Journal of Forensic Sciences*[1] in July 2002.

In 1987, 19-year-old Darci Pierce was tormented by the fact that she was adopted. "She wanted to have a child to prove that she was a better mother than her adoptive or biological mother," forensic psychiatrist Dr. Michael Stone told *The New York Times*.

She lied to her husband and convinced him that she was pregnant. She stashed surgical instruments and medical books in her home. When her husband left for work one day, she told him she was going to the hospital, where she was scheduled to have labor induced. Then she drove over to the Kirkland Air Force Base in Albuquerque, New Mexico, and parked outside of the prenatal clinic.

Darci wasn't preparing to enter the clinic, though. She didn't have an appointment with a doctor there—or anywhere. She was lying in wait, looking for the right pregnant woman to walk out of the building and into her trap.

She didn't have to wait long. There she was. She was young—just 24 years old. She was obviously far along in her term—eight months pregnant, in fact. Her name was Cindy Ray.

[1] *Journal of Forensic Sciences*, July 2002, Vol. 47, No. 4. "Newborn Kidnapping by Cesarean Section": Ann W. Burgess, R.N., D.N.S.; Timothy Baker, Ph.D.; Cathy Nahirny; John B. Rabun, Jr., ACSW.

Darci forced her into her car at gunpoint. She used her left hand to steer. With her right, she aimed the muzzle of the gun straight at the stomach of the trembling, tearful expectant woman. Darci's plan was to take Cindy to the home Darci shared with her husband. At her own house, Darci had the equipment and reference books she needed to perform a cesarean section.

Darci was forced to change her plan. She couldn't go home—she realized as she approached the residence that her husband's car was in the driveway. He wasn't supposed to be at home, but there he was. Darci drove past her house with one hand still aiming the gun at her captive. Could she take the baby without her books and tools? she wondered. As bizarre as it sounded, Darci simply did not believe she had a choice any longer. Her mind raced as she tried to decide on an alternative location.

She drove out to an isolated area of the high desert in the East Mountains. She strangled Cindy until she lost consciousness. She dragged the limp form out of the car. Without the surgical instruments she'd planned to use, she had to improvise. She rummaged through her car, but could not find a knife or a pair of scissors. The only sharp objects she could find were the car and house keys hanging from a ring.

That was what she used. She had to push down hard to get the keys to cut through the skin—even harder to sever the muscles. It was difficult. It was ugly. But Darci managed to cut Cindy open enough to remove a live baby girl. Darci abandoned Cindy on the side of the road—leaving her to bleed to death on the hard ground.

Darci now had the baby she wanted—but somehow she needed to get her hands on a birth certificate so that she could successfully claim that the child was her own. She drove to a car dealership where a friend worked and told her that she had just delivered a baby. The friend took her to the local hospital where Darci told her husband earlier in the day that she was scheduled for labor induction.

The physician took one look at her and, skeptical of her story, performed the gynecological exam. Darci's pant legs were covered with mud and blood. Something did not look right. When he performed his examination, his suspicions were confirmed—there was no physical evidence that Darci had given birth to a baby. He called authorities and she was taken into custody.

At trial, the defense argued that in addition to borderline personality disorder and narcissistic personality disorder, Darci suffered from atypical disassociative disorder that made her incapable of controlling her actions—and thus she was legally insane at the time she committed the crime.

The prosecution expert—the renowned Dr. Phillip Resnick—agreed with the defense on the first two disorders, but argued that, rather than suffering from disassociation, she had antisocial personality disorder. His diagnosis was not consistent with an insanity defense.

The jury split the difference, finding her guilty but mentally ill. Their decision sent Darci to prison, where she would remain for at least 30 years. At that time, her condition would be reassessed, possibly giving her a change in status.

In Brownsville, a Texas town on the border with Mexico, an abduction occurred in 1992 that was strange enough to be chronicled in the "News of the Weird" column in newspapers across the country. Rosa Botello met Laura Lugo, a 27-year-old pregnant woman, at a social gathering in town. Rosa introduced Laura to her sister Paulyna, who lived in the nearby town of McAllen. Paulyna claimed that she, too, was pregnant.

The two sisters cultivated a friendship with Laura. They included her in shared meals, shopping excursions and hours of conversation. Laura was 8½ months pregnant and living from one welfare check to the next when the sisters made her an offer that was too good to be true. She needed a prenatal checkup they told her. It will be our gift to you, they said. The sisters took Laura to an appointment at the Brownsville office of Paulyna's obstetrician, Dr. Mauricio Bierstadt.

After a cursory examination of Laura, the doctor spoke with the two sisters. He then asked them all to meet him in his office across the border in Matamoras, Mexico. Laura was confused by this and was at first reluctant to go. Rosa and Paulyna made light of the doctor's instructions and promised they would all go shopping afterward, thus luring Laura across the border.

In his Mexican examination room, Dr. Bierstadt gave Laura an injection that caused her to lose consciousness. While she was under, Dr. Bierstadt performed a caesarean section and gave the baby to Rosa and Paulyna. When Laura regained consciousness, nurses told her that her baby was gone. And the Botello sisters were gone, too.

Laura battled for two years to regain custody of her child. It was a difficult fight, since Paulyna—through bribery or trickery—was able to obtain a birth certificate showing that the baby boy was her biological child and his father was a Mexican drug lord. Laura maintained her constant refrain that she gave birth to that baby until the courts decided to re-solve the issue by ordering DNA testing.

The genetic analysis was still in process when the Botello sisters changed their story. Now, they claimed that the baby was not the biological child of Paulyna, but it was rightfully her baby just the same.

Laura approached them, they said, because she wanted to get an abortion. Instead of giving her the money for that pro-cedure, they convinced Laura to allow them to pay the med-ical expenses of carrying the child until birth if she would give the baby to them after it was born. Laura agreed, they claimed, to let Paulyna have the infant.

In 1994, DNA testing proved conclusively that the 2-year-old the Botellos named Jorge Daniel Alaniz was Laura's biological child. The court awarded custody to her. The punishment handed to the sisters was light. Prior to trial,

Paulyna spent 62 days sitting in a Mexican jail awaiting extradition to the United States. Aside from that time, neither of them faced any imprisonment. They both received a sentence of 3 years probation.

Laura enjoyed the reunion with her baby for eleven weeks. She disappeared on December 21, 1994. Her charred skeleton—riddled with bullets—was found by authorities six months later. In October 1997, an informant told police that a woman named Janet Ramirez was with Laura Lugo when she died.

When Janet was arrested on theft charges in April 1998, police questioned her about the death of Laura Lugo. She confessed to being involved in the murder. Janet was the mistress of Randall Ledbetter, a U.S. Border Patrol agent based in Arizona, and saw Laura as her romantic rival for Ledbetter's affections.

Janet's first plan to eliminate the competition was to make Laura look bad in Ledbetter's eyes. Janet—identifying herself as Laura Lugo—made threatening phone calls to Ledbetter's wife. The calls frightened her and she told her husband. Ledbetter was infuriated and determined to make the calls stop. That was when, according to Janet, Border Patrol Agent Ledbetter hired Brownsville Police Officer Roberto Briseno to kill Laura. Janet claimed to be present when Briseno received his payment from Ledbetter—a handful of bullets and $1,000 cash.

Janet and Briseno convinced Laura to go with them to a remote location under the pretense of a rendezvous with Ledbetter. There, Janet said, Briseno shot Laura six times.

Janet Ramirez pled guilty to murder and received a 20-year sentence. She testified at the trial of the two former officers of the law.

The jury, however, did not find Janet's testimony credible. They acquitted both Roberto Briseno and Randall Ledbetter. Justice was not something Laura Lugo ever received—not during her short life and not even after her death.

* * *

Jacqueline Williams, of Addison, Illinois, a suburb of Chicago, had three children, but she wanted one more. Her boyfriend Fedell Caffey wanted a boy. Her cousin Laverne Ward knew where she could find one. Debra Evans, his former girlfriend and the mother of his 19-month-old son, Jordan, was pregnant again—with someone else's child—and the baby she carried was a boy. Debra had already picked out a name—Elijah.

Jacqueline set the stage for the abduction. In April 1999, she began a charade of pregnancy. She said her baby was due in August. After friends threw a baby shower for her early in that month, she moved the due date forward to October. That month passed and still Jacqueline had no baby.

On November 1, she told her probation officer that she gave birth that day. On November 9, she told him that she named her son Elijah. But Jacqueline still didn't have a baby.

Early in the evening of November 19, Jacqueline checked to make sure that Debra Evans' live-in boyfriend James Edwards had left the house for work. Then Jacqueline left her home with boyfriend Caffey and cousin Ward.

Debra Evans didn't know she had anything to fear that night at 9 when she opened the door and let the trio into her apartment. She sat on the love seat chatting to Jacqueline about her pregnancy and about her three children: 10-year-old Samantha, 8-year-old Joshua and her little toddler Jordan.

Ward interrupted their small talk and flashed $2,000 cash in Debra's face. He wanted to buy the baby she was carrying. Debra refused. Ward towered over her, yelling in her face. Debra would not budge—she would not sell her baby. Ward pulled out a small automatic handgun and shot Debra in the head.

Caffey and Ward dragged Debra off the love seat onto the floor between the small sofa and the coffee table. While Jacqueline looked on, Caffey used a pair of poultry shears to slash Debra's belly, cutting some of her small intestines on his way to her womb. Ward kneeled by Debra's head, stabbing her in the neck with a knife.

Caffey pulled the baby out of Debra's body and cut the umbilical cord. Little Elijah wasn't breathing. Caffey was ready to drop him and run. Jacqueline snatched the infant from his hands. She blew into his nose and mouth. The newborn wailed and began to breathe on his own.

While Jacqueline dressed Elijah, Caffey and Ward headed down the hall to the children's bedroom. They stabbed and slashed Samantha's throat seven times. Joshua ran from the room screaming that the bad men were hurting his sister. Jacqueline dropped a Winnie the Pooh baby blanket on top of Debra's body, but it was too small to conceal the lifeless form from Joshua. At the sight of her, he ran into the bathroom and threw up.

Jacqueline headed for the back door with the baby in her arms. Joshua threw his arms around her legs and begged her not to leave him in the house with the bad men. She took him out to the car with her. For a few brief moments, the little boy felt safe. Then they were joined in the car by Caffey and Ward.

Little Jordan—not yet 2 years old—was left home alone with only the bloodied bodies of his dead mother and older sister for company. When James Edwards got home from work, the bewildered little boy met him in the kitchen. A frantic Edwards checked his wife and her daughter for any signs of life—then he called 9-1-1.

Jacqueline dropped Joshua off at the home of her friend Patrice Scott to spend the night. She told Patrice that Joshua's mother was shot in a drug deal and was in the hospital.

Joshua whimpered in his sleep all night long and cried as soon as he awoke.

"Are you worried about your mama?" Patrice asked.

Joshua nodded.

"Don't worry. She's at the hospital. She's okay."

"No. No she's not. She's dead. My sister's dead." He told Patrice about the burglars who broke into his home. As the shocked woman listened, he told her the names of the men who killed his mother and sister.

Patrice confronted Jacqueline when she arrived around 9 that morning with a newborn infant in her arms. Jacqueline called Joshua a liar, but the little boy stood his ground and sealed his fate.

He could identify the attackers. They could not afford to let him live. Jacqueline forced him to swallow iodine in an attempt to poison him. She and Caffey tried to strangle him with a rope, but Patrice intervened and saved his life—for a few minutes more.

Out in the car, Jacqueline held Joshua while Caffey stabbed him to death. They dumped his body ten miles away behind a building in Maywood.

Jacqueline Williams and Fedell Caffey were found guilty and given the death penalty. Laverne Ward received a life term in prison. But the death sentences would not stand.

In January 2003, Governor George Ryan made a startling pronouncement about the ultimate punishment: "Because our three-year study has found only more questions about the fairness of the sentencing; because of the spectacular failure to reform the system; because we have seen justice delayed for countless Death Row inmates with potentially meritorious claims; because the Illinois death penalty system is arbitrary and capricious—and therefore immoral—I no longer shall tinker with the machinery of death.

"This is a blanket commutation. I realize it will draw ridicule, scorn and anger from many who oppose this decision."

He wrapped up his address with a quotation from Supreme Court Justice Potter Stewart: "The imposition of the death penalty on defendants in this country is as freakish and arbitrary as who gets hit by a bolt of lightning."

That week in Illinois, 171 prisoners sat on Death Row. Ryan granted full pardons to four men, reduced the sentences of three others to the point that they would be released within weeks, and commuted the death sentences of 160 men and one woman—including Jacqueline Williams and Fedell Caffey—to life imprisonment without the possibility of parole.

The families of many of the victims were outraged. Among those speaking out was Sam Evans, Debra's father: "All he talked about is the death penalty issue, which, for this governor, is to be expected. He is not very concerned with individuals, just with issues."

The people of Illinois still argue whether Ryan was motivated by politics or by principle.

Twenty-nine-year-old Felecia Scott of Tuscaloosa, Alabama, had two boys before her hysterectomy in 1994. The next year, she was living with a new boyfriend, Frederick Polian. Felecia was convinced that she needed a baby to maintain this relationship. She told her partner and her mother that she was pregnant.

Felecia befriended an expectant 17-year-old, Carethia Curry. She told the teenager that she was pregnant, too. Using this bond she earned the girl's trust.

Carethia was in her ninth month on January 31, 1996, when Felecia invited her out for pizza. After dinner, the two women returned to Felecia's apartment to talk and relax.

Instead of socializing, Felecia shut the door and pulled out a gun. She shot Carethia twice in the head. The pregnant girl was fatally injured, but still alive when Felecia kneeled beside her with a knife and a pamphlet opened to a diagram of a cesarean section. Felecia cut Carethia from breast bone to pubic bone. She made a bisecting cut and removed the baby from the dying girl's body.

Felecia crammed a dying Carethia into a plastic garbage can and sealed it shut with duct tape. When Frederick Polian arrived at the apartment, Felecia showed him the newly born baby, telling him she'd just given birth at home. She asked him to dispose of the trash can she filled with the bloodied towels and blankets she'd used during the birth and in the clean-up afterward.

Felecia took the baby to a hospital in Birmingham for a checkup. Frederick drove outside of that town and dropped the makeshift plastic casket into a fifty-foot ravine.

The next day, Carethia's family contacted police and reported her missing. The authorities questioned Felecia, since she'd been the last person to see the missing girl alive. When they asked her about the infant in her possession, she showed them the paperwork about "her" baby's birth from the Birmingham hospital. She made it through that interview, but knew it was only a matter of time before investigators uncovered her medical history and learned she was incapable of giving birth to a child.

She plotted her defense and started putting the pieces into place. On February 8, she visited her father and told him the story she concocted. She had been riding in a car with a friend, she said. When the police stopped the vehicle, she fainted. When she came around, she told her father, the police were gone, her friend was gone but there on the car seat was a baby.

Her father didn't believe her story, but before he could figure out what to do, the police were knocking at his door. They had an arrest warrant for Felecia.

On March 14, 1996—six months after Carethia's disappearance—her body was found in the ravine. Prosecutors filed murder and kidnapping charges against both Felecia Scott and Frederick Polian.

At his trial, Frederick admitted to disposing of the garbage can, but insisted that he did not know a body was inside it. He was adamant that he had nothing to do with Carethia's murder. He was acquitted on the murder charges, but found guilty of kidnapping.

Felecia had a separate trial where her attorneys claimed that Frederick was responsible for the death of Carethia. Felecia, they said, only went along with Polian's plot because she feared for her life. Felecia Scott was found guilty on all charges and, although the death penalty was possible, the jury recommended life without parole.

Josefina Saldana was sterile from a hysterectomy performed ten years earlier. She never told her new husband about this procedure. He wanted children and, despite her physical limitations, she was determined to give him what he wanted.

On September 13, 1998, Josefina called the Fresno home of Eliodor Cruz and his wife, Margarita Flores. The baby Margarita was expecting would be their sixth child. On the phone, Josefina claimed to be a charity worker with a gift of baby supplies. The next day, Josefina arrived and Margarita drove off with her to go to a warehouse where Margarita believed she was going to pick up free baby furniture and a one-year supply of diapers.

It was only supposed to be a twenty-minute trip. When Margarita had not arrived home nearly two hours later, Eliodor was concerned. He called Margarita's family and together they contacted the police.

The day after Margarita's disappearance, Josefina walked into a hospital with a dead fetus. She told the nurse that she'd given birth in her car.

That same day, Serafin Rodarte, a farm worker who rented from Josefina, saw an adult body wrapped in a carpet on the property. He told police about his discovery two days later—but by that time, the body was gone. A few days after talking to police, Serafin was found hanged inside his one-room cottage. It appeared to be an act of suicide.

Three weeks later, pieces of Margarita's body were found mixed in with trash on a remote hillside near Tijuana, Mexico. Authorities arrested Josefina and charged her with double murder. The prosecutors decided not to seek the death penalty. The jury found her guilty in 2001 and sentenced her to life without parole.

Two days after her conviction, Josefina used up the blades on six disposable razors to shave her head. She braided some of her hair and put it in a small package to mail. She wrote four additional letters.

She picked up a tube of lipstick and wrote on the stainless-steel mirror in her cell: "Fresno, may God forgive you. Babies, I am not a murderer. I love you."

She tied a sheet around her neck. She tied the other end to

the ceiling and stepped off of her cot. Jailers found her dead body hanging in her cell.

Erin Kuhn, an emergency room technician, was 31 years old, divorced, the mother of one son, and a cancer survivor. To save her life, doctors performed a hysterectomy. Now incapable of conceiving any more children, she desperately wanted another.

She attempted to adopt children three times without any success. When her 17-year-old unmarried niece, Kathaleena Draper, became pregnant and agreed to let her aunt adopt the baby, it seemed like an answer to Erin's prayers.

In March 2000, Kathaleena moved from Las Vegas to Sacramento to live with Erin. An attorney drew up adoption papers. Erin bought a crib, a car seat, diapers and piles of baby clothing for the anticipated child. Erin even selected a name for the baby boy—Jeffrey.

Then in June, Kathaleena changed her mind. She wanted to keep her baby and she wanted to move back to Las Vegas. Erin drove her niece back to Nevada. In a room at the Lazy N Motel in Fernley, the two argued. Erin insisted that Kathaleena had to give her the baby. She had taken care of her, taken her to the doctor, made all the arrangements. Kathaleena could not back out now, her aunt demanded. Kathaleena did not wither under Erin's barrage. The child was hers, Kathaleena said, and she would keep it. Without warning, Erin snapped.

She shoved a latex glove into Kathaleena's mouth and forced it down the pregnant girl's throat. As Kathaleena asphyxiated, Erin made a horizontal cut in her abdomen. Layer by layer, she cut through Kathaleena's body until she could remove the baby.

Little Jeffrey was in distress. Erin performed CPR for nearly an hour before she realized her efforts were in vain. She put the infant in a garbage bag, sealed it shut and set it in the front seat of her Ford Taurus. She wrapped her niece's body in a blue plastic shower curtain and loaded her into the back seat.

She dumped the bag containing Jeffrey in the high desert south of Fernley near Silver Springs on the side of the highway. Erin drove back to Sacramento with Kathaleena's body in the car. She dumped her on the side of the road on the outskirts of town.

Erin was arrested when Kathaleena's remains were found. Later, Erin directed authorities to the location where she had abandoned Jeffrey's tiny body. To avoid the death penalty, she pled guilty to the first-degree murder charge in the death of Kathaleena and to a second-degree murder charge for causing the death of the baby. Erin Kuhn was sentenced to life without parole.

At the age of 13, Michelle Zonka discovered her father's body in the garage. He had committed suicide by inhaling carbon monoxide fumes. The trauma of that event turned Michelle from a cheerful child to one who was somber and petulant. As soon as she was old enough to leave home, she did—severing the emotional connections with the rest of her family. In 1983, Michelle married an Iranian immigrant. Relations were so strained that her family did not know he existed until after the divorce.

After leaving her husband, she spent the next five years adrift. She lived in at least eight different cities before she settled down in the town of Ravenna in Portage County, Ohio.

She was locked up in the Portage County jail in Shalersville from April through October 1994 after pleading guilty to receiving stolen property. Thomas Bica, a friendly, mentally slow, shy man who was overweight and suffered from a stutter, was a corrections officer for the Portage County Sheriff's Office who'd started working the day shift at the jail on September 26 of that year. Not the most romantic way to meet, but Thomas was smitten just the same.

After Michelle's release from jail, she was diagnosed with a condition that causes the uterine wall to thicken and harden, making a successful pregnancy an unlikely prospect. It didn't stop her from marrying Thomas Bica, a man who wanted to have children with her and raise a family together.

In December 1999, she told Thomas she was pregnant. Soon she was wearing maternity clothes. She played it up for all it was worth, urging relatives to rub her belly, and squealing at them to come feel the baby kick. Except for Thomas, who was convinced he felt the movement of the baby on more than one occasion, no other family members got their hands on Michelle's tummy in time to feel a foot kick, an elbow jab or a fetus roll to a different position. But they still believed her. After all, Michelle showed them ultrasound images of the baby. Who could doubt scientific proof?

Michelle decorated a room, bought lots of baby bottles and installed a monitor in the kitchen that connected to the nursery. She and Tom toured the birthing facilities at Akron General Medical Center. They discussed their baby's future.

She even sent a letter to her employer allegedly written by her doctor:

> Due to medical complications caused by advanced pregnancy, Mrs. Michelle Bica has been cautioned to exercise complete bed rest until her next appointment in this office on August 2, 2000. Ms. Bica should have someone with her 24 hours a day due to the nature of her illness. She should not drive any kind of motorized vehicle, lift heavy items or climb stairs. As always, this office would like to thank you for your patience in this matter.

The letter was signed by Dr. Richard L. Mitchell. Dr. Mitchell had never once examined Michelle, and the signature on it did not match his handwriting.

On August 26, family members threw a baby shower for Michelle, enabling her to stockpile even more supplies. She was close to term and they thought she was showing. Michelle was a heavyset woman and that helped a lot in her deception.

She and Tom were shopping in Wal-Mart when they met

Theresa and Jon Andrews in the baby department. The two couples chatted about their pregnancies and discovered that they lived just a few blocks apart. Before that encounter, Michelle said that her baby was a girl, due in early September. After learning that her neighbor's baby boy was due at the end of the month, Michelle changed the gender and delivery date of her fantasy pregnancy to match Theresa's real one.

On the morning of September 27, Michelle Bica called Theresa Andrews and asked her about a Jeep the Andrewses had advertised for sale. Theresa rode in the Jeep while Michelle made a test drive. No one knows what excuse Michelle made, but Theresa was not alarmed when Michelle pulled the car into the driveway of her own neat white home with its impeccable yard. Theresa accompanied Michelle to the house and just inside the back door that opened onto the laundry room.

Michelle pulled out a .22-caliber handgun and shot Theresa in the back. The bullet pierced her left lung and lodged in her heart—killing her instantly. Using a kitchen knife, Michelle quickly slashed her victim's stomach and removed the baby boy.

She then dragged Theresa into her dirt-floor garage. She buried the body in a shallow grave and covered it with some of the gravel that she ordered for delivery a few days before.

She cleaned up the trail of blood that ran from the laundry room to the garage. She drove Teresa's Jeep to a parking lot a block away from the Andrewses' home. Putting the keys to the Jeep in her purse, Michelle walked the few blocks back to her house.

After finishing her cover-up, Michelle called her husband at work and told him she delivered the baby at the hospital, but they sent her home right away because of a tuberculosis scare.

"Why didn't you call me before you went to the hospital?" he asked.

"My water broke. I was in too much pain. It all happened so fast," she said.

Thomas was disappointed that he had not been present for the birth, but he believed every word Michelle said. For five days, she kept up the deception that the baby was hers. Neighbors who came to see the baby worried about Michelle—her solemn demeanor made them fear she was suffering from post-partum depression. She talked more about the disappearance of Theresa than she did about her baby—she seemed to be obsessed with her neighbor's plight.

Tom, on the other hand, was bursting with pride. His joy was apparent as he prattled on about his newborn baby boy.

Police did not look at Michelle as a person of interest in Theresa's disappearance until they reviewed telephone records. They questioned Michelle about cell phone calls made to the Andrews home on the morning Theresa last spoke to her husband Jon. Michelle's responses were evasive and contradictory.

They ended the first interview with red flags flying high. They returned to her home the next day to question her further. They stepped out of their cars and walked up the sidewalk. As they neared the front door, they heard the sound of a gunshot followed by Tom shouting, "Michelle! Michelle! Michelle!"

Police found Michelle Bica dead from a gunshot wound to her mouth inside the couple's bedroom. She used the same gun to commit suicide as she had used five days before to put a bullet in the back of her neighbor's head.

The Andrewses' baby was not harmed—she was sound asleep in the second-floor nursery. Tom was confused and distraught. He lost his wife. He lost the baby that he thought was his own. He denied the possibility that his wife could have done such a horrible thing. He insisted that she gave birth to that baby and the baby was his.

Then things got even worse for Tom. He discovered his wife's credit card bills. Without his knowledge, she had accumulated $40,000 in debt. He had to sell his home to take care of the bills.

Jon Andrews brought a lawsuit against Tom in August

2001—suing him for millions of dollars. Jon was convinced that Tom had to be aware of Michelle's horrid plot. He even suspected that Tom could have been involved in Theresa's murder.

A 1997 report in Tom's personnel file had described him as "not intelligent," "exceptionally gullible" and "out of touch with commonsensical type of behavior." Tom appeared less like Michelle's accomplice and more like one more victim of her narcissistic personality.

Effie met 21-year-old expectant mother Carolyn Simpson at the Creek Nation casino in Okemah, Oklahoma. Effie was a regular patron there. Carolyn worked at the bingo tables. Since February 2003, Effie had told everyone that she was going to have a baby. It was now December and still no delivery.

Carolyn was six months pregnant when she left work on December 22 and met Effie in the parking lot. Effie promised her a crib and some clothing for her baby. She climbed into Effie's car and they drove away.

Effie stopped the car in an unpopulated area and shot Carolyn in the head. Using a knife and razor blades, she removed the 6-month fetus from the young woman's body. She dumped Carolyn's remains in a field near Lamar.

Effie brought the baby home and told her husband that she had given birth on the side of the road. The next day, Effie drove thirty miles to a hospital in Holdenville. She walked through the doors with a dead baby boy in her arms.

Effie was transferred to a hospital in Tulsa. An examination there made it clear that Effie had not given birth to the child. Because of that, she was taken into custody as a material witness in the disappearance of Carolyn Simpson.

On the day after Christmas, a hunter stumbled across Carolyn's mutilated body. Effie faced two charges of murder and a charge of kidnapping. She was eligible for the death penalty.

In November 2004, Effie Goodson was found mentally incompetent to stand trial.

All these stories had much in common with the tragedy that befell Bobbie Jo Stinnett. Each perpetrator was driven by a deadly desperation for a child. All were consumed by a narcissism so entrenched that the real mother was no more than a womb—a tool for the perpetrator to satisfy her desire.

Each used subterfuge to get close to her victim. Some of them were driven by a more warped impulse than the one held by a typical baby kidnapper. They planned every detail. They did not just want another woman's baby. They desired to possess a baby who never looked into the face of any other woman—one whose sole maternal imprint was their own.

As inexplicable as it sounds, every one of these women thought that everyone else would believe that the baby belonged to her alone.

In Kansas, Lisa Montgomery listened carefully when the news of Effie Goodson's crime broke in the neighboring state of Oklahoma in December 2003. It was a timely story for Lisa. There were cracks in the foundation of her marriage. She could feel it in the soles of her feet. Her relationship with Kevin was in danger.

She believed that she needed a baby to keep her man. She was incapable of pregnancy and thought that was so unfair. In her mind, she needed a baby more than anyone. She refused to allow her inability to conceive to stand in the way. She wanted to keep Kevin—she would keep Kevin—at any cost.

She analyzed Effie's every action. She used her observation of Effie's errors as a template of what not to do as she planned and carried out the commission of the same crime.

She thought it was so simple. She believed all she had to do was avoid Effie's pitfalls. She would not steal a baby too immature to survive without medical attention. She would not select a victim who lived near her own home. She would do everything right, she thought. She felt she would get away with the perfect crime.

22

On the crisp Friday evening of December 17, 2004, Sheriff Espey approached the microphones again. "What we're going to do tonight—this might be the last chance that law enforcement is going to be able to talk to the press. The reason is, when the attorney general's office—the U.S. Attorneys—get involved in the case, it actually becomes a turnover to the court system, and they'll get control of that. We've done our job up to this point.

"I want to thank you people for being there for us and helping us with the Amber Alerts. And for having the patience you have had and not tormenting me and coming in and demanding that I speak to you.

"The first forty-eight hours is very, very crucial in the Amber Alert. This case went twenty-three hours before we located this little girl. And at this point, we're going to cancel the Amber Alert—we're that confident that we have the girl that was taken from Skidmore.

"I also want to thank the people who helped me on this. The department couldn't have done it alone. The Major Case Squad, comprised of law enforcement all over northwest Missouri, the Buchanan County CSI—these people were very well trained and they were very good. They helped us out at the crime scene over in Skidmore.

"The FBI—there were seven or eight FBI agents that came in and tremendously helped us because of some of the computer stuff that was a little out of our control. They knew about that and were ready to dig right in and get that going. Public Safety Officer Randy Strong—he started from hour one and stayed with us through this whole thing. Most everybody here has been up continuously and we've run leads all night long and we've continued to run leads today.

"When this Amber Alert came out—that's the greatest thing that ever happened to law enforcement and to our children. We took an anonymous tip that came from several states away from here that gave us some information that led us to Kansas and this location. And we may have not ever gotten that; we may not ever recover the little baby if the Amber Alert system was not put in place.

"It's hard for me to accept this. Nobody here could ever perceive this taking place—to have a fetus taken out of someone's womb and then doing an Amber Alert to try to find the child.

"It's inconceivable. I'm overwhelmed with the fact that we're going to be able to get this baby back."

Sergeant Sheldon Lyon, spokesman for the Missouri State Highway Patrol, stepped up to the mike after the sheriff ceded his place. "This is a great day for law enforcement in northwest Missouri," he said.

The case was now in the hands of United States Attorney Todd Graves of the Western Missouri District of the federal court system. Graves was a Northwest Missouri local. He grew up on a farm in Tarkio in Atchison County.

After completing his undergraduate work at the University of Missouri at Columbia, Graves earned a law degree and a master's degree in public administration from the University of Virginia in 1991.

His legal experience included service as an assistant attorney general for the state of Missouri, followed by a short stint in private practice before he was elected in 1994 as prosecutor for Platte County—whose boundaries encompassed a portion of Kansas City, Missouri. In this capacity he was the youngest full-time prosecuting attorney in the state. He was re-elected four years later.

On July 30, 2001, President George W. Bush nominated Graves as the top federal law enforcement official for the Western Missouri District. He was confirmed by the Senate in October. In this position he was responsible for a district covering more than 40,000 square miles with an approximate population of 2.4 million. He oversaw the functions of three offices with a full-time staff of fifty-five attorneys and sixty other employees.

Although high-profile criminal prosecutions drew the most attention, the bulk of the office's work involved civil matters—defending the federal government against legal claims made by individuals and groups and serving as collection agents for debts owed to the government.

Graves lived with his wife and four children north of Kansas City on a 270-acre homestead. The farm had been passed down through generations of his family since 1867.

Zeb Stinnett saw his infant daughter for the first time on Friday evening. He gave her the name he and Bobbie Jo agreed upon—Victoria Jo Stinnett. The meaning of Victoria—winner or conqueror—made it a prophetic choice for this survivor.

Medical personnel checked and double-checked the health of the baby in the neonatal intensive care unit. DNA tests confirmed her parentage. Zeb returned home to northwest Missouri with his baby girl on Monday, December 20.

Zeb did not, however, return to Skidmore and the cozy bungalow on Elm Street. He could not bear to live in the house where his young wife died. He moved in with his mother in the nearby town of Maitland in Holt County. There, Victoria Jo slept in a crib once used by her 10-year-old uncle, Tyler Harper.

Zeb took a twelve-week paternity leave to adjust to his new role as single father and to grieve for the loss of his wife. He found homes for some of Bobbie Jo's rat terriers, but he kept her two favorites, Belle and Tipsy.

In Melvern, Lisa's coworker at Casey's General Store was stunned by the news of what had happened. She felt betrayed—after talking with Lisa for hours about her pregnancy, she believed it was real. Now she knew it wasn't, and to make matters worse, she heard about Lisa's contention that this pregnancy started as a pair of twins, and other false claims.

She was surprised that she'd fallen for Lisa's lies. She knew the family and was well aware that truth was not their constant companion. If Lisa seemed to be telling the truth, the coworker said, maybe that was because she had also convinced herself. Lisa, she said, had thought that Kevin wanted—and needed—another baby. After that, it was easy for Lisa to delude herself into believing that she would deliver one to him.

For two days straight, the FBI questioned Kevin Montgomery. They tried every method they knew to break down his story, trip him up or catch him in a compromising contradiction. Finally, they were convinced. Kevin really was as clueless as he claimed.

While Kevin sat in the hot seat, crime-scene investigators hunted for clues in Lisa's red Toyota. They found a three-inch serrated paring knife they suspected was used to perform the amateur caesarean. They also seized a black ski mask with red-and-white trim, a pair of work gloves, latex exam gloves, a dirty dish towel, a bottle of surgical prep solution and a photograph of a squirming litter of newborn rat terrier puppies.

* * *

Hardened crime-scene investigators returned to their head-quarters in St. Joseph—their professional shells shattered in the wake of this horrendous, intimate homicide. On the scene they suppressed their emotions, but back at the station their reactions tumbled out. They talked about the case for hours—easing the stress of an investigation that hit too close to home.

The media plunged into the history of caesarean abductions. Many were shocked at the number of cases that went unnoticed in the years before. They also struggled with the linguistics of the story. Should they describe the unborn child taken from Bobbie Jo Stinnett 25 a fetus or a baby? And at what point did the transformation take place? And how?

Amber Alerts were for children, yet editors were insisting on the use of the word "fetus" to describe the subject of the Amber Alert. The Associated Press managed to wrap the whole process up in one linguistically confusing sentence:

> Montgomery, 36, confessed to strangling Bobbie Jo Stinnett of Skidmore, Missouri, on Thursday, cutting the fetus out of her body and taking the baby back to Kansas.

Pro-life spokespersons and columnists made the most of the confusion. They scolded the media—whom they suspected of pro-choice sympathies—for wanting to have it both ways. Either the fetus was nothing more than a clump of cells to be destroyed at the whim of a woman, or the fetus was a baby—a human life with value and meaning. They also used the opportunity to chastise organizations who opposed legislation granting protection to "*in utero* children" by allowing assault and homicide charges to be levied in their name.

Pro-choice advocates pointed out the importance of choice—Bobbie Jo's choice—to have a baby. Feminists proclaimed that Lisa Montgomery's actions demonstrated the pervasive pathology of a society where a woman was only valued for her role as a breeder.

While some nitpicked over life-and-death matters, others used the crime as fodder for sarcastic humor, usually aimed at Kevin Montgomery. *The Pitch*—a Kansas City weekly alternative newspaper—devoted its first "Kansas City Strip" column after the crime to "providing tips to help rural Kansas men figure out whether their wives are really pregnant."

The writer, Tony Ortega, expressed mock sympathy for Kevin's cluelessness. He wrote that they understood how Kevin "had no freakin' idea that something was terribly wrong about his wife Lisa's 'pregnancy,'" while the whole time she was not really expecting but rather plotting how to pay an allegedly murderous, baby-takin' visit to Bobbie Jo Stinnett.

"After all, there's a lot on the mind of the average rural Kansas man.

"Winterizing his car. Wondering why the Chiefs sucked this year. Playing the Lotto."

He also ridiculed Lisa's choice of the Long John Silver's parking lot to meet her husband with the baby: "even the most distracted Kansan would know that such an occasion calls for a meeting in the parking lot of a Red Lobster, at the very least."

What this essay ignored and what many people did not understand was that Kevin was not alone in his ignorance. Many men—from highly educated engineers to backwoods farmers—have accepted the claim as an article of faith when their wives informed them that they were expecting children.

The history of infant abductions was riddled with men who were intelligent, but naïve about pregnancy and the mysteries surrounding birth. At the same time, these men were manipulated by women who could read them very well—each one a woman who knew her man would react in the manner he did and stay by her side.

Another reason their pregnancy ruses were effective and easily maintained over months was that the relationship was already dead. When interviewed after abductions, the men expressed no affection, no love, no physical passion for their spouses. It was all duty—their responsibility to stay with the woman until the baby came.

If she did not want to be touched or seen naked during her supposed pregnancy, that was fine with him. He had no more sexual desire for his partner and, therefore, couldn't care less.

It had always been easy to love a baby, and the wife used that to her advantage. She involved her husband in her nesting activities—buying clothing and diapers, decorating the nursery, reading passages aloud to him from baby books. She urged him to touch her belly and feel the baby move. He was averse to physical contact with this woman, so he touched quickly and then retreated, accepting her word that he felt the growing life inside her. Each step bound him closer to a child whom he thought was his own.

Before Reverend Wheatley knew that a young woman's death in Missouri would leave a trail of blood that went through his church, he prepared his Sunday sermon. The title of his message, "A Baby Changed Everything," would prove to be eerily prophetic. The message, however, had nothing to do with the tragedy that unfolded over the next couple of days; it was about the birth of Jesus in a stable in Bethlehem. He did not alter his speech to include the nightmare that crept into their community that weekend. It was the last Sunday before Christmas and he wanted the service to be a time of worship and praise to the Lord for his gift of his only son. Even in the face of the horrible news, Reverend Wheatley wanted to maintain the integrity of that special day. He wanted his parishioners to remember—now more than ever—the real reason for the season.

On December 19, with a numb mind and aching heart,

Kevin Montgomery attended the First Church of God in Melvern with his parents and three of his stepchildren: Desiree, Chelsea and C.J. He handed a written statement to Reverend Wheatley.

In the pulpit, Wheatley read Kevin's statement to the congregation:

> As everyone here knows, this hasn't been a very good week. This is going to be a long and difficult road for these families to walk down, but if we look and hold out our hands, God is there to lead the way. Please keep Lisa, the kids, and I in your prayers. Our sympathy also goes out to the family of Bobbie Jo Stinnett.

Except for this missive from Kevin, Reverend Wheatley avoided any mention of the tragedy in their midst. But when a congregant rose and took his place at the front of the church to deliver the meditation for communion, it was obvious that he was inspired by recent events. The passage he read was all about forgiveness.

As the choir sang "The First Noel," Desiree buckled over and shook as she sobbed. Moisture gathered in Chelsea's eyes, but she refused to allow the tears to fall. Parishioners gathered around the Montgomery clan after the service. They offered enveloping hugs and whispered words of encouragement in their ears.

Skidmore Christian Church was an emotional quake zone that day, too. The congregants spent the service alternating between tears of sorrow and of joy. They grieved for Bobbie Jo and rejoiced for Tori Jo. They lifted prayers to the heavens for them both.

The same day that Victoria Jo returned to her home state, Lisa Montgomery made her first appearance before a judge in federal court for the Kansas District. The moment Lisa had crossed the Missouri state line into Kansas with the baby, her offense became a federal crime. Kidnapping was the primary charge—the murder of Bobbie Jo was committed in the commission of that crime. For that reason, she faced charges in federal court for the Kansas district. She looked drained and pasty in her blue jumpsuit and oversized glasses.

Two public defenders, Charles Dedmon and Ron Wurtz, represented her. They told Magistrate Judge David Waxse that their client would oppose moving the case to federal court in Missouri. Since the crime originated in one of the sixty-six counties covered by the Western District Court's jurisdiction, the prosecutors needed to try the case there.

The defense team demanded a preliminary hearing and an identity hearing in Kansas District Court first. They also asked for a gag order. The judge denied that last request with a reminder to attorneys on both sides that it would be prudent to limit their comments to the media.

Judge Waxse read Lisa her rights and the list of charges against her. He informed her that she could be sentenced to death or to life in prison, and could be fined as much as $250,000.

Except for one brief glance at Kevin, Lisa hung her head low and kept her eyes focused on the federal complaint lying on the desk in front of her. Even knowing what she had done, it had to be shocking and mind-numbing to a woman who had no criminal record to read the heading on the document before her. "*United States of America, Plaintiff* v. *Lisa M. Montgomery, a/k/a Darlene Fischer a/k/a Fischer4kids, Defendant*." The odds in that contest must have seemed daunting—she had to feel as if she stood alone against the whole world. And she had to know that out of all the documents created to date, the most damning passage was the penultimate paragraph of the eight-page FBI affidavit:

> After being advised of her constitutional rights and having waived those rights, Lisa Montgomery thereafter confessed to having strangled Stinnett and removed the

fetus. Lisa Montgomery further admitted the baby she had was Stinnett's baby and that she had lied to her husband about giving birth to a child.

The judge approved Lisa's move from Wyandotte County Jail in Kansas City, Kansas, to the federal detention facility in Leavenworth. She was due back in court in three days—on Thursday, December 23.

Outside of the courthouse, a bewildered and distraught Kevin Montgomery spoke to the media: "I had no idea. My heart ain't just broke for me and Lisa and her kids. It's them, too," he said referring to the Stinnett family a state away. "My family has suffered a tragedy, but I am not the only family. This has to be as hard or harder on them as it is on me. I sure hope they get as much support from their church and community as I have, because we are all going to need it. That was a precious baby. I know."

23

Family and friends helped Zeb make arrangements for a funeral service on Tuesday, December 21 at 2 P.M. at the Price Funeral Home in Maryville. The night before, TV satellite trucks converged on the funeral chapel, picking out prime positions to park their vehicles overnight. They wanted to be as close to the action as possible, even though the media was banned from entering the funeral home or driving into the cemetery.

At midday, the mourners began to arrive—hundreds of them—dressed in Kawasaki jackets, brown work clothes, cowboy hats and jeans, and in more typical funeral dress clothes.

By 1:45 that afternoon, all the folding chairs the funeral home possessed were in use. Even though reporters and news photographers were kept away, there was an overflow crowd that filled two rooms, spilled into the entry, down the stairway and out into the biting wind and 20-degree temperatures.

The solemn crowd shifted places every few minutes to allow
everyone a turn near the sanctuary.

Surrounded by a bounty of blooms, the rosy bronze casket was adorned by a simple garland of lilies. Bobbie Jo
rested on a bed of creamy satin, in a purple dress with a tiny
angel pin fastened to the wrist of her right sleeve. Her an-
gelic face—no longer filled with the cheerful animation it
once possessed—radiated a peace and serenity unmarked by
the pain she had endured at the hands of her attacker.

The logistics of accommodating 400 mourners caused a
delay in the commencement of the service. The overflow
crowd was silent—a silence so still it pierced your ears. The
heavy quiet was punctuated by subdued sobs and sniffles.
The service opened at 2:15 with a selection of organ hymns.

Bobbie Jo's baby was not in attendance at her mother's
funeral, but everyone there had seen the photograph of the
peaceful infant sound asleep—her pink cheeks aglow, her
baby lips drawn up like a Christmas bow.

Reverend Hamon approached the pulpit and read the
Twenty-third Psalm. He said, "This is one of those times in
life when you would like to have the right words, but I don't
know what to say. This is one of those times when you can't
figure it out at all, and words fail. I've been a preacher for
fifty years, and I've seen some terrible things. But this has
got to be the apex."

He then turned everyone's attention to the happiest day of
Zeb and Bobbie Jo's life—their wedding day. He pulled out
the note Bobbie Jo wrote thanking him for officiating at that
service and read it out loud.

He quoted from Isaiah 55:8–9: "For my thoughts are not
your thoughts, neither are your ways my ways, declares the
Lord. As the heavens are higher than the earth, so are my
ways higher than your ways and my thoughts than your
thoughts." Then he added, "God did everything he did because he loves us. Bobbie Jo gave her life for her baby because she loves her."

He recalled a friend of his who hung on to scaffolding

suspended nine feet above the ground, clinging with all his might with just his fingertips. There was nothing he could do but ask for God's help before his fingers lost their grip and he plummeted to the ground. "And there comes times in life when we have to externally seek help. This is one of those times, because now, this family has been dropped off of a 900-foot cliff."

He asked that everyone say a prayer for Zeb Stinnett and his baby girl. "There won't be a day or a night that they don't miss Bobbie Jo. The only explanation I can think of is that God has a special place for her."

The mourners sobbed and clutched a program containing the words to the song "Merry Christmas from Heaven." After thirty minutes, the service was over.

The attendees, with red-rimmed eyes and grief-numbed minds, drifted out of the sanctuary and to their cars. As one woman left the chapel, she snapped at a cameraman, "You just can't get enough, can you?" Just days earlier, the media was being praised for the instrumental role they played in the safe recovery of Bobbie Jo's baby. Now that they were no longer needed, they were treated with scorn.

Most of the people who attended the service joined the funeral procession. A train of cars and pickup trucks more than a mile long followed the hearse on its fourteen-mile journey up State Route 113 to Newton's Corner in Skidmore.

Turning left, they traveled through acres of farmland and across the one-lane, steel-truss bridge that forded the icy Nodaway River. They climbed a steep incline to Hillcrest Cemetery, a small five-acre swath of land cut out of the surrounding fertile fields. The oldest marker, dated 1865, stood at the site of the grave of Sonia Walker, a 4-year-old girl. Passing the stone of that young child reminded many of their gratitude that today they were burying Bobbie Jo alone—not with her baby by her side.

High on the hilltop, the steady wind was even more ruthless. It reddened cheeks, froze teardrops and chapped lips.

The air was so crisp, it hurt to breathe. Mourners gathered under two blue canopy tents at Bobbie Jo's final resting place. Around them stood haphazard rows of tombstones—more souls rested there than now lived in Skidmore.

Zeb stood by his wife's casket and read the Twenty-third Psalm as he choked down his sorrow. In ten minutes, this portion of the service was over. Many stopped before they left to shake Sheriff Espey's hand and thank him for finding Victoria Jo.

After the service, family and friends crowded into the Newton Community Hall where the fire department prepared and served supper. The emotions of those in attendance swung from sadness to fury and back again.

One of the mourners, Jo Ann Stinnett, staggered under an oppressive mantle of pain. She received a call from her stepson, Zeb's father, Danny Stinnett, on December 16. He had told her Bobbie Jo was dead and the baby was missing.

None of it seemed real to Jo Ann until the funeral—the fourth for a family member she'd attended that year. In March 2004, her son died, and she'd also lost two of her siblings to cancer.

The horror of Bobbie Jo's brutal death flashed before her eyes and dragged her down an ugly road to her traumatic recent past. It was not the first time violent death drove this family to its knees. It was the third time in just four years. The déjà vu Jo Ann felt was debilitating.

24

Babe and Jo Ann Stinnett's granddaughter Wendy was born on January 19, 1975, to Randy and Sandra Gillenwater in Fairfax, Missouri. By October 2000, Wendy's life in Skidmore was in shambles.

For the past six years, she lived with her boyfriend, Gregory Dragoo. Half of Dragoo's life was consumed by untreated substance abuse. His problem with addiction began when the parents of a friend in Denver, Colorado, introduced him to drugs. When Wendy moved in with him in 1994, she, too, consumed large quantities of illegal substances. The expense of their drug habit mired them in abject poverty. The ensuing depression and hopelessness of their lifestyle, accompanied by the drug abuse, intensified the negative characteristics of Dragoo's personality.

He was a violent, abusive and controlling man. He isolated Wendy from family and friends. He kept her secluded in their home. Often, he took her clothing or shoes with him when he went out to ensure that she would not leave the house.

For months he beat her, covering her body with bruises. Wendy told no one of her horrible plight—not even her mother. She just took more drugs to help her forget.

On October 16, 2000, Dragoo's violence went over the top. He pounded on Wendy until she fell to the floor. She did not fight back during this assault, but in a fit of defiance she spat in his face.

He kicked her supine body with his bare feet, slamming them into her so hard that he bruised the tops of his own feet in the process. He fractured six ribs on her right side, eight ribs on the left, lacerated and collapsed one lung, lacerated her liver and caused additional internal trauma and bleeding.

As she gasped for breath, he poured dishwashing liquid down her throat. He picked her up, carried her out the door and dumped her lifeless body in the backyard where he continued to pummel her.

A neighbor heard a noise and went outside to investigate. He saw Dragoo standing over a woman stretched on the ground at his feet. The neighbor returned to his home and pounded 9-1-1 into his cordless phone. Gregory Dragoo settled on the front steps of his home at 406 E. Elm Street and waited for the arrival of law enforcement.

An ambulance pulled up in front of the house at 1:45 that afternoon. Paramedics rushed to Wendy's side and began their assessment. Her pupils were fixed and dilated. She had no pulse or respiration. Her face and neck were swollen. Hemorrhage bloomed red on her neck and scalp. She had two black eyes and bruises all over her face, chest, abdomen and arms. Her skin was cold to the touch. The emergency medical technicians believed she was clinically dead when they arrived at the scene. Nonetheless, they provided forced respiration and CPR to Wendy as they transported her to the St. Francis Hospital in Maryville.

She was unable to breathe on her own, and medical personnel pronounced her dead at 5:13 P.M. Her death was the result of blunt force chest and abdominal trauma.

Police slapped cuffs on Dragoo and took him into custody. He said that he was enraged at Wendy and totally out of control. He admitted to hitting her, kicking her and throwing her into a wall. He said that Wendy never struck back. When he'd carried her outside, he said, he believed that she was dead.

A few blocks away, Jo Ann Stinnett answered a knock on her door. Jo Ann had noticed the commotion and asked, "Do you know where the ambulance is going?"

"That is why I'm here," her neighbor said. "I came to tell you your granddaughter Wendy is near death. She has a slight heartbeat, but it does not look good." In fact, by that time, Jo Ann's granddaughter had already been declared dead.

Wendy's mother, Sandra Stinnett Gillenwater, was devastated. Her daughter's face was battered beyond recognition. She was able to identify her only by the rings she wore. Sandra felt guilty for not checking up on her daughter—for not forcing her way into Wendy's life before it was too late.

Wendy's funeral service was held on October 20 at the Price Funeral Home in Maryville. She was laid to rest at the Hillcrest Cemetery, where Bobbie Jo Stinnett (another resident of Elm Street) would be buried four years later.

In June 2001, Sandra presented a check for $1,700—money she and other volunteers raised for the Wendy Gillenwater Memorial Fund—to the Nodaway County Family Violence Council. The donation was earmarked for a shelter for the victims of domestic abuse.

On August 15, 2001—the day Dragoo was scheduled to face prosecuting attorney David Baird and a panel of his peers—he waived his right to a jury trial and pled guilty to murder in the second degree. Circuit Judge Roger Prokes accepted his plea and ordered the Missouri Department of Probation and Parole to perform a pre-sentence investigation.

After receiving their report, the judge handed down punishment for Gregory Dragoo on November 6, 2001. Wendy's family, Dragoo's attorney and Dragoo's family presented statements. Judge Prokes then sentenced Dragoo to the maximum possible sentence for second-degree murder—life imprisonment in the custody of the Missouri Department of Corrections. He also ordered that Dragoo would receive credit for time served, pay the per diem jail costs to the facility where he was incarcerated since his arrest and pay $68 to the crime victims' compensation fund. The judge also determined that there was no probable cause to believe the defendant received ineffective assistance of counsel.

In Skidmore, just a few steps from Newton's corner, a small tree stood surrounded by a circle of rounded bricks. Before it a plaque read:

IN MEMORY OF WENDY
GILLENWATER, 1975–2000.

25

Months before the courts meted out justice for Wendy Gillenwater, another tragedy struck Skidmore and the Stinnett family. Jo Ann's grandson, 20-year-old Branson Perry, disappeared.

Branson was born on February 24, 1981, to Bob and Becky Perry. When his parents divorced, Branson lived with his father. His younger brother, Phillip, lived with their mother.

Branson and his dad had a close relationship. They hunted for Indian artifacts, fished, camped and hiked together. They took classes in Hapkido, a Korean art of self-defense. Father and son learned the arm and leg joint locks, weapons use, throws, kicks, hits and nerve pressure techniques. Each earned a black belt in this martial art.

Branson was a blond-haired, blue-eyed boy with a passion for homemade peach pie. His baby face made him look younger than his years. He graduated from Nodaway-Holt

High School in 1999—one year before Bobbie Jo Stinnett.
He attempted to enlist in the Army, but failed the physical
because of a racing-heart condition.

On April 7, 2001, Branson visited his neighbor, Jason
Bierman, who gave him an unidentified drug. In an intoxi-
cated state, Branson danced naked, shaved his pubic area
and participated in sexual activity with Jason.

The next day, Branson stammered out the story to his
father, Bob. Branson feared the humiliation and embarrassment he would suffer if the encounter became public knowledge. Bob knew his son had homosexual tendencies and
suspected that he'd had sex with other men, so he wasn't en-
tirely surprised. Nonetheless, after hearing the pain in his
son's voice, he became angry at Jason for drugging, then using his son. Bob entertained dark thoughts of killing his
neighbor, but never acted upon them.

On Wednesday, April 11, 2001, Branson's father Bob was
in the hospital in Maryville. Branson's grandmother Jo Ann
Stinnett and his friend Gena Crawford came over to the
Perry place to clean up the all-male home on Oak Street in
preparation for Bob's return.

Gena saw Branson out in the front yard talking with two
guys who were replacing the alternator in Bob's car. She
called out the upstairs window and asked, "Branson, what are
you doing?"

Branson said, "I'm going to put away the jumper cables,
then run out for a bit. I'll be back in a few minutes." He
tossed the cables into the shed and then walked off the property. Gena never saw him again.

Early Thursday morning, Jo Ann visited Bob Perry in the
hospital. "Did Branson come to see you last night?" she
asked. When Bob said he hadn't, Jo Ann was alarmed. Since
Bob went into the hospital, Branson visited him every night.
She shrugged off her worry, not wanting to create anxiety in
Bob while he was ill.

As she drove back to Skidmore, Jo Ann's anxiety grew.

She stopped in at the Perry home and found the doors open. Nothing, however, appeared to be missing. Her fear cranked up another notch.

Where could she look for her grandson? She called his mother, Becky, but she hadn't seen him either. She couldn't check with an employer—roofer Royce Clements laid Branson off some time ago, and except for a short stint with a traveling petting zoo, Branson hadn't found another job. He didn't have a serious girlfriend. He didn't own a car.

Jo Ann went home and called the Perry house often over the next few days, but never got an answer. She called around town, but no one had seen Branson. She bounced from anger at Branson's irresponsibility to dread that something bad had befallen him. In addition to worries about foul play, Jo Ann was concerned that Branson's racing-heart condition caused a medical crisis. On April 16, Jo Ann and Becky and Bob Perry filed a missing persons report.

Nodaway County Sheriff Ben Espey sent out ground search parties that scoured a fifteen-mile perimeter of Skidmore. The Missouri Highway Patrol and the Drug Strike Task Force aided in the search. They combed every farm, field, vacant building and pond they encountered. They found no sign of Branson. Dogs were not used because a rain had fallen after Branson's disappearance—any possible traces of his scent had already washed away.

In the next month and a half, the sheriff's department interviewed hundreds of people. With reluctance, Gena admitted that Branson smoked weed and used amphetamines. A family member told investigators that Branson had a bottle of Valium in his possession the afternoon, he'd disappeared. Down in St. Joseph, Branson's acquaintances in the drug trade submitted to lie detector tests. Nothing. No one had seen Branson Perry.

Bob Perry offered the best lead. He suggested that Branson—embarrassed by his sexual encounter with the neighbor—may have hitchhiked to Kansas City to visit his close friend Mike Lemon. Other members of Branson's family found that difficult to believe. They were not aware that he had ever hitched a ride anywhere. True or not, investigators questioned Mike. That led, too, led nowhere.

Quite a number of leads centered around the suspicion that Branson was involved in the local drug trade. Those tips claimed he was killed because he owed a lot of money to another dealer or because he was about to turn others in to law enforcement for illegal drug activities. Every trail followed ended with no resolution and no sign of Branson.

Branson was gone and his trail was as cold as a bitter December wind. Desperation drove the family to psychic Joyce Morgan in Kingston. Joyce visited Skidmore on June 1 and June 6. She talked to people who knew Branson and stopped by the places he frequented.

Joyce claimed that she saw Branson dead and his body was not in the Skidmore area. She said she had a vision of every moment of torture and abuse inflicted on Branson. She could not, however, share the details with the family because they were far too horrific.

She offered leads to Sheriff Espey, however. He dutifully followed up each one with care. Although later revelations would indicate there might be some truth buried in Joyce's vision, none of it had enough clarity to provide an obvious trail to the missing young man. Despite valiant efforts, each lead went nowhere.

In December 2001, Becky Perry established a $5,000 reward fund for any information resulting in the safe return of Branson or for the successful prosecution of any guilty parties. Shortly before the one-year anniversary of his disappearance, friends in Becky's hometown of Oregon, Missouri, pulled together a chili supper, raising $1,000. Becky added that money to the reward fund.

In that first year, Becky distributed 1,300 fliers about her son. They were plastered in store fronts, on telephone poles, in restaurants—anywhere and everywhere—throughout Northwest Missouri and into Iowa, Kansas and Nebraska. She also made an online appeal.

> I never thought before, but tonight I received an email of someone looking for their son. I thought that it wouldn't hurt for me to try also.
>
> My son, Branson Kayne Perry, is 20 years old and has been missing since April 11, 2001. He left his home in Skidmore, MO telling a friend that was there that he would be right back. No one has seen or heard from him since. This is not a typical behavior of Branson. He has never been out of touch with his family or friends for more than a day or two at the most.
>
> I am asking, pleading, begging for your help please! Please forward to everyone you know and if anyone anywhere has seen him please contact me. As a parent, you can have no idea what I am feeling unless you have gone through the same thing. I can't begin to tell you the pain and agony I feel everyday and night. I just want to know that he is safe. The police have exhausted all leads they have and nothing. No one saw anything. No one knows anything. No one has heard from him.
>
> Please help me, Please. And if you haven't seen him, please say a small prayer for his safety. I thank you from my heart and God Bless you.

In late March, new leads came in to law enforcement. Patrols took cadaver dogs to four locations in Missouri: two in Burlington Junction and two in Quitman. And still the family waited—for Branson to walk through the door or for Sheriff Espey to deliver the dreaded news that his body had been found.

A break came from an unexpected source—the FBI's

Candyman investigation. Special Agent Mickey Roberts headed the probe into child pornography on the Internet. His work led him to Michael Adam Davidson, a third-year medical student at the University of South Alabama who was arrested and charged in March 2002. Among the many sexually explicit images involving children found when they analyzed Davidson's seized computer were two .mpg streaming video files—one depicting a sex act between an adult and a minor, the other a short movie of a man dying as his throat was cut. Davidson sent a thank-you email to a man identified as BuggerButt remarking that the throat-slitting file was "too short."

They also found an ominous online chat dated a month earlier between MickPower2134—Davidson's screen name—and BuggerButt, an apparent sexual predator who had the disgusting and revealing habit of referring to his victims as "it." They hoped it was just sick fantasy, but feared it was all too real.

He wrote, "I just had a second 'oh shit' experience."

"Tell me about it," Davidson urged.

"One was on a Wal-Mart missing board."

"Ha Ha, tell me more."

"I saw something that I knew was not going to be returned and was definitely missing though the facts mentioned there were sanitized greatly over what it told me happened," BuggerButt wrote, referring to the poster of Branson Perry he'd seen in the store. On it the simple facts of Branson's disappearance and his life were a resource of ridicule for BuggerButt, who wove a tale of familial abuse that led Branson onto the predator's path.

"I am curious," Davidson pushed. "Why don't you tell me all about it, I would be fascinated."

"Well, that is not all of it. Just had the second one. A friend was telling me about a site on the net that sifts facts and fiction—all the Internet hoaxes, chain letters, all that shit. So I went to it and looked at the item he referred me to. I cruised the site under missing persons and what to my wandering eyes did appear but another like the Wal-Mart wall," he wrote, referring to the site where he'd read the appeal made by Branson's mother.

"So you met him?"

"Oh, yes," BuggerButt answered, "and it did not just disappear. There was more involved or so it told me."

"You've got to tell me from start to finish, I am most intrigued."

"Skidmore is a very small town. Was famous for their being silent when a bully guy was killed by someone that they all knew but refused to give up. Still haven't. But that's another story that has nothing to do with me. This kid was gay."

BuggerButt went on to defame the character of the Skidmore boy and his family. He claimed that he picked him up hitchhiking on an interstate.

"Were you looking at the time, or did you just have an opportunity you could not refuse?" Davidson asked.

"Opportunity," BuggerButt replied. Then he played coy about providing any more details. "Just realized that this is the first time I have ever given any definable details to anyone. Not smart of me and a bit scary," he wrote.

"Are you scared?" Davidson asked.

"Just a bit squeamish—means that someone actually has some details."

"You would not have told me if you did not think you could trust me."

"No offense," BuggerButt wrote, "but that kind of thing can be a fatal mistake."

"So why did you tell me?"

"I have to accept that my natural instincts are correct."

"You have no reason to fear me," Davidson reassured him. "I don't know what else I can say or do."

"I know. It is just me. Was hit with one of the 'oh shit' moments," BuggerButt continued. "You have no idea how it felt that time in the fucking Wal-Mart. And then today when I saw that site."

"How good it felt?"

"Hard to say. Good in some great thoughts and memories—but also a knot in the stomach. Most are throwaways. No one gives a shit. No one is even looking."

Davidson reminded him, "Remember your philosophy. Prey and predators."

"Most prey I have found is not worth looking for."

"Do you have regrets on this one? Because you fear getting caught? Or you feel sympathy?"

"Neither," BuggerButt tapped out on his keyboard.

"Good."

"Maybe some fear of seeing something that comes forward if pics are out there. Usually no one knows they are missing or no one is going to come forward with 'I saw . . .' "

"Did anyone see what happened?"

"I don't think so. But sometimes people do but it means nothing. You have to operate on the premise if you look like you know what you are doing, people don't notice. If you 'sneak,' people wonder what you are up to. If you stop and pick up someone and look like it is normal, then they don't think squat."

"I agree. Your best method is to act as if it is nothing out of the ordinary. Will you continue telling me about what happened after you picked it up?" Davidson asked.

"It took a beer after it smoked a joint. Got very drunk— was not used to drinking," he wrote. "Got it drunk enough that it agreed to take a pill."

"What type of pill?"

"Phenobarb," he wrote. "Became most compliant."

"An anti-convulsant, a barbiturate?"

"Yeah. It really slows down muscle control along with the beer. It was warm enough that I detoured to do an Ozark overnight. Its clothing was added to the campfire I built to knock off the night chill. Damned shoes fucking stink and smoke when burned."

BuggerButt wrote that after undressing the blond Skidmore boy, he tied him to a tree. He then revealed the depths of his depraved mind as he recounted the unspeakable physical torture he perpetrated on the young Branson Perry.

The normal imagination cannot even conceive of the disgusting abuse that was a warm memory to BuggerButt. And the medical student on the other end of the Internet conversation reveled in each moment.

Besides the repulsive physical acts BuggerButt performed, he also recited with even more pleasure the joy he found in the mental torture of Branson and of all his victims.

"You can do it willingly by telling it you are going to let it go if it does what you want. Hope springs eternal until you smash it."

"Very nice technique," Davidson wrote.

BuggerButt admitted that his greatest pleasure was when he so thoroughly broke his victims that they were willing to commit suicide to escape from him. He said when he first started commiting these crimes, he used drugs for courage.

"You did drugs?" Davidson asked.

"But I figured out it was just a crutch to let me do what I wanted. So did not use when I did one. Made it much more real since I know it is me and what is in me—not some drug. In some ways, it no longer matters what I do with the body. It is the mind I love to destroy and break. Actually, I am disappointed even if it suffers horribly if I don't break it totally.

"When it begs me to kill it—it doesn't always happen—but when it does I know it is broken. Each mind is different and learning that mind is the real game to tearing down barriers. Destroying hopes. Building false ones."

"And do you deny its request?"

"Actually, yes," BuggerButt wrote. "It becomes so powerless that it can't even determine its own death. But it comes anyway. I like destroying values and morals and religion—making it feel totally helpless."

BuggerButt then talked about the victims that he drove to such extreme despair that they committed suicide. "The youngest that offed itself was maybe 14. Oldest was probably 40's," he wrote.

"How do you manage a 40 yr old grown man alone?"

"With its legs and arms broken. Actually it is the older teens and 20's that are the hardest and have to be kept tied or cuffed the entire time."

"But probably most enjoyable when you break them," Davidson interjected.

"Don't go so far on broken feet, either. Remembered that from scout camp where I worked for some summers."

"I was a boy scout."

"Scouting taught me many skills. Some I am sure they are not proud of."

"Like knot tying, 'be prepared,' " Davidson suggested.

"Well, I have been thinking about doing it for real."

"I hope so," BuggerButt wrote. "I want you to know the feeling. The power."

"I figure I can easily get access to drugs to sedate," said the medical student. "Wrap it in a sheet and put in my trunk to leave no evidence on the car."

"Other details you need to deal with also but when you are ready, I will walk you through it."

"I appreciate it, my mentor," Davidson wrote.

"I want you to be successful."

"Right, I want success."

"Your ability to think about things that can be found is good. So, you need to first find a place to do it. Then the place to dispose of it."

"I think the key to that is randomness."

"Ideally where it won't be found. Gator swamps are nice if you could get to one easily . . . but I think that is still too far."

"Not really," Davidson wrote.

"Water does a real number on evidence if you had to use the gulf. Gators take food into their dens and let it rot first. Rarely are things found."

"I have to find a secluded area to conduct the torture."

"Your first will have to be fast and to the point. Usually best. Longer scenes are fun but you don't have your senses honed yet. Some very intense but only a few hours of pain is what I would recommend."

Returning to his lurid description of the death of Branson Perry, BuggerButt wrote: "It was an eighteen-hour project actually." He explained how he had to clean up the scene by sifting the ashes to remove anything identifiable that had not been incinerated and dispose of the body in a manner that guaranteed it would never be found.

In other correspondence, he claimed he eviscerated Branson's body, thrown the internal organs in a ditch and then tossed the body into deep water. Without the guts inside to decompose, he explained, the body would not bloat and therefore, would not float to the surface.

"I want to have that experience and soon," Davidson wrote.

26

Special Agent Roberts contacted the Nodaway County Sheriff's Department and inquired about any missing children in the Skidmore area. There was only one person who matched the description in the chat log. And Branson Perry was such a good match to all the facts that Roberts knew the disgusting conversation on Davidson's computer was no baseless fantasy.

The FBI served a court order on America Online to obtain information about the actual identity of BuggerButt. In short order, Roberts had a name for Davidson's correspondent—Jack Wayne Rogers. Rogers lived in Fulton, a town of 12,000 in central Missouri.

Located in the rolling foothills of the Ozark Mountains, Fulton was an area of lush, green beauty. The nature-infused serenity of state parks was just a short drive in any direction. Fulton was also the home of the internationally

known Winston Churchill Memorial and Library and of a
section of the Berlin Wall that was moved to the campus of
Westminster College and transformed into a sculpture com-
memorating Churchill's 1946 Iron Curtain speech.

Fulton, as the seat of Callaway County, was the site of a
bizarre Civil War footnote. Callaway County citizens saw
the approach of Union soldiers and initiated talks which led
to a mutual ceasefire agreement with the United States.
Upon their success in diplomacy, they renamed the county
the Kingdom of Callaway—an appellation that they still use
in the county to this day.

Fulton was also the model for the town depicted by native
Henry Bellamann in his novel, *Kings Row*. The 1942 movie
based on this book starred Ann Sheridan, Robert Cummings
and Ronald Reagan.

Jack Rogers added a new chapter to the history of Fulton.
But it was a tale the other citizens would like to erase.

Detective Clint Barnett of the Fulton Police Department
confiscated and searched the trash that Jack Rogers left on
the curb for pickup in January and February 2003. He did
not find any evidence of his involvement in child pornography in the garbage, but he did obtain proof that Rogers
resided in the home—that information was important to obtain a search warrant.

Roberts and his team of investigators, including officers
from the Fulton Police Department, descended on his ordinary-
looking two-story white frame home at 707 Nichols Street on
March 18. What they found inside was not ordinary in the
least.

In the search of the property, the investigative team seized
handcuffs, sex toys, and bondage and torture equipment—
collars and limb restraints, gagging devices, leather whips
and full latex body suits that covered from head to foot with
only a small hole for breathing—from Rogers' Chrysler
Town & Country minivan.

Inside the house itself, Agent Roberts found clamps,

cauterization tools, bandages, sharpened knitting needles
and the plastic cup from an athletic supporter pierced with
nails that pointed inward.

The biggest horror of all was the documents and photographs found on the computers seized from Rogers' residence.
Child pornography consumed byte after byte of space—
more than a thousand images in all. There was also a wealth
of images depicting mutilation and torture. The words
Rogers wrote on his computer were chilling, too. The torture
and murder of many males was described in graphic detail
under the online pseudonyms of BuggerButt, ohailsatan and
extremebodymods.

The horror that even one individual this depraved existed
was compounded by the knowledge that there were many others willing to listen—and to enjoy—his lethal ravings. And
those men were not crazed individuals living on the edge of
society. These were men who lived seemingly respectable, ordinary lives and worked in professional positions—one was
the vice president of patient services at a hospital.

On April 9, the Missouri Highway Patrol, led by Sergeant
David Merrill, did a simultaneous followup search at the
home and business of Jack Rogers. The specific mission of
this excursion was to find evidence linking Rogers to the
murder of Branson Perry.

They seized Rogers' minivan, which they searched a
month earlier. This time, they found a necklace with a turtle
claw pendant—just like the one Branson's grandmother Jo
Ann Stinnett said he'd worn for good luck. From inside his
home, they seized a scalpel kit from the nightstand beside
his bed, and from the basement they took a green box containing sexual paraphernalia. A tool box with more sex toys
was located in the travel trailer on his property.

Roger owned and operated Decker & Decker employment service on the second floor of the Kelly Plaza complex
in Columbia—a city about midway between Kansas City
and St. Louis.

An employee of Decker & Decker claimed she spotted Rogers on several occasions running off copies of stories featuring acts of sadomasochism, mutilation and homosexuality that he had written under the pseudonyms Jolly Rogers and BuggerButt. She said that he mailed these stories to prison inmates.

At his business, officials seized his computers and a manual describing a "gender nullification procedure," a phrase used to describe surgical castration. They discovered a room there that Rogers had converted into a recreation area for the practice of the Bondage–Domination–Sado-Masochist lifestyle.

The forensic analysis of his computer confirmed that Rogers had accessed the TruthOrFiction website where Becky Perry's plea for help for her missing son was posted. One photo on a confiscated compact disk showed Rogers dipping a severed penis and scrotum into his mouth. Another showed discolored male sexual organs artfully arranged like haute cuisine on a white dinner plate with a green-and-pink flowered edge. The plate sat on a checkered tablecloth. There were also before and after photographs of a man who had undergone the removal of his sexual organs at the hands of Jack Rogers.

It also showed that Rogers had deleted material from his company computer the day after the federal search of his home. It showed an additional document dump on April 4. Rogers did not stop at altering his own computer files. He obtained the password to the Yahoo account of Barry White—one of his correspondents. White did not have a computer of his own, but communicated with Rogers through public computers, and all of his emails were kept on the Yahoo server.

Rogers had written to him about cutting off a man's fingers and storing them in a plastic bag in his glove compartment. He sent White various digital images, including one of Rogers standing by a roiling pot. Rogers' commentary with that photograph bore a repulsive remark: "You would not taste anything quite as good as boiled testicles." These organs Rogers claimed he obtained when he surgically castrated other men. Rogers deleted all of this material from White's account.

While doing the search at Decker & Decker, Sergeant Merrill and Corporal David Rice interviewed their suspect. "We're investigating the disappearance of a boy from Skidmore, Missouri. Have you ever been to Skidmore?"

Rogers said that he had not.

Merrill then asked, "Have you ever been on an Internet website related to Branson Perry or stumbled onto information regarding Branson Perry?"

Jack Rogers denied several times that he had ever seen any of that information. "I wish I could help you, but I do not know anything about the missing runaway."

Rice said, "We did not say that Branson Perry was a runaway. Where did you hear that he was a runaway?"

Jack Rogers shifted in his chair displaying a restless discomfort. For a moment he was silent. Then he said, "I just assumed he was a runaway."

Merrill pulled out a copy of the TruthOrFiction website labeled "Exhibit 2" and showed it to Rogers. Jack looked at it and denied ever going to that site on the Internet.

"Look carefully at this photo of Branson Perry on the website. Look at this photograph, too. Have you ever seen this boy?"

Rogers denied ever seeing his picture before. "I surfed the web often and may have come across this webpage, but I never met Branson Perry in person. And I never had any contact with him in person or on line. Never seen the boy, never talked to anyone about him."

Then Merrill handed Rogers a copy of the Internet chat log that included Rogers' discussion of meeting, torturing and killing Branson Perry.

Rogers swallowed hard and shifted in his chair again. His face flushed and small tremors flashed around his eyes. "It appears that I may have been playing a game with someone," Rogers said.

"What do you mean, Jack?" Merrill asked.

"I think I better have an attorney."

With that, the questioning of Jack Rogers came to an end.

Roberts arrested Rogers on just the child pornography charges on April 10, 2003—one day before the second anniversary of Branson's disappearance. In Jo Ann Stinnett's yard in Skidmore, the yellow ribbons of hope had faded to a stark white.

For the last three years, Rogers had worked as the lay pastor for Manse Bellflower Presbyterian Church in Bellflower—a tiny town of 400 just thirty-four miles up the road from Fulton. He was appreciated by the congregation for his lively, inspirational sermons.

The congregation reeled at the news of his arrest. They cancelled their annual Vacation Bible School—a project led by Rogers. They feared that some of the 50–75 children who attended the session in previous years may have been harmed by the monster in their midst.

The revelation that a small number of members held a closely guarded secret about Rogers' past rattled them again. In 1992, Rogers was director of Ecumenical Ministries, a cooperative organization of Catholic and Protestant churches providing community services programs. He was also involved in the Great Rivers Council Boy Scouts and took a group of boys on a camping trip to Arizona.

Rogers was identified in a sting operation involving the controlled delivery of child pornography conducted by the United States Postal Inspection Service. A search warrant led to the discovery of pornography throughout Rogers' home and in his Corvette, including visual depictions of minors performing sex acts. They also found a photograph of Rogers with his penis nailed to a wooden board and another with his testicles clamped in a bloodied vise.

Rogers pled guilty to the interstate transportation and receipt of visual depictions of minors engaged in sexually explicit conduct. He admitted in court that he paid a Houston supplier $55 for a magazine and photographs of child pornography. He received a 4-month jail sentence and 3 years of probation. Those in the know at the church overlooked this transgression because Rogers convinced them that he was innocent and others set him up for a fall.

With his new arrest on child pornography charges, the full truth of his previous criminal record was revealed. The parishioners in his Presbyterian church were appalled and chagrined.

On November 12, 2003, a subdued Rogers—in an orange jumpsuit and Velcro sneakers—pled guilty to ten of the eleven counts in the indictment issued by the grand jury. In a plea agreement, he offered four statements of fact. He admitted there were images of child pornography on the two computers removed from his home. He agreed that images and video of the same had been on the two computers and compact disk removed from his office. He said that he'd sent four emails with an attached photograph of a minor engaged in sexually explicit conduct. Finally, he admitted that he sent three emails with an attached photo of male genitalia on a dinner plate and another picture of an adult male after his penis and testicles were removed.

"Is your mind clear?" U.S. District Magistrate Judge Scott Wright asked Rogers.

"I have a bit of a headache this morning, but yes, sir," Rogers replied.

When the judge pressed him for an admission of guilt, Rogers equivocated. "I believe I would probably be found guilty." Then, he added, "I want to get this behind me."

That last comment made Branson's mother, Rebecca Perry, more outraged than she'd ever been in her life. The man who probably stole her son's life was looking to his own future. In her mind, he did not deserve a future at all.

27

Two days after Rogers' court appearance, Sergeant David Merrill of the Missouri Highway Patrol sought and received authorization for another search. This time the specific purpose was to seek any evidence of human remains or biological material.

In the affidavit, Merrill presented his assessment of the nature of Rogers' perversions.

> In the investigation of Jack Rogers, the offender's collection reflects not only his specific sexual interests with regard to desired age and gender characteristics (underage or youthful males), but also with regard to particular sadomasochistic sexual practices (among them impalement, castration and cannibalism.) Individuals who have a demonstrated willingness to turn their fantasies into reality by acting on them may be more likely, having overcome the internal and external inhibitors such as guilt

and fear, to continue acting on those desires and possibly
to escalate. Investigation has confirmed that Jack Rogers
indulged in at least one of his sexual interests, specifically, he caused pain and suffering by performing surgical castration on an individual. Jack Rogers also claims
to have consumed the male genitalia removed during
surgery. It must be noted that of the small number of
cases reviewed by the FBI's Behavioral Analysis Unit involving cannibalism, it has rarely been seen without an
associated psychiatric history, which frequently does not
rise to the legal definition of insanity.

Jack Rogers has identified himself as a sexual sadist
during online conversations and described an event in
which he claims to have abducted and tortured a young
adult male hitchhiker. Since Jack Rogers has already acted
on other sadomasochistic fantasies, it increases the risk
that this abduction scenario actually occurred. An individual who is sexually aroused by adolescent males and also
sexually aroused by the pain and suffering of others, may
victimize young-looking adults or actual child victims
with whom he can satisfy some or all of his sexual desires.

Additionally, he noted that when an individual persisted
in criminal activity when they have reason to believe the
conduct had come to the attention of law enforcement—as
Rogers did—they were particularly dangerous.

This is desire-driven behavior characterized by a persis-
tent pattern of behavior involving a willingness to commit significant time, money and energy in furtherance of
the specific sexual preferences, often resulting in multiple offenses.

On November 17, Sergeant Merrill returned to Nichols
Street with Officer Pat Horn and his dog, Sabra, and Officer
William Albright and his dog, Cinder. The dogs sniffed the
four flower beds in the backyard and the paving stones on the

patio. They did not alert at those areas, but when they approached the Crown Royal Silver Eagle travel camper, Sabra made digging motions indicating the presence of human biological materials. Cinder alerted at the same location. From the trailer, they seized couch cushions, a backpack, two plastic tubs and tent items and took them to the highway patrol lab in Jefferson City for processing and analysis.

The officers got busy digging. First, they tackled the four flower beds. Each seventy-two-square-foot bed was above ground and held in place by wooden timbers stacked two feet high. Then they removed the paving stones on the patio and dug beneath them. They tore the backyard apart, but to their great disappointment, they found no incriminating evidence buried in there. Investigators still did not have the proof they needed to charge Rogers with the murder of Branson Perry.

On April 28, 2004, Rogers returned to court for sentencing. The prosecution put six witnesses on the stand to support their position that an extreme sentence was warranted on Roger's child pornography charges.

One of those witnesses was nursing student Madison Abercrombie. After online contact, Michael—now Madison—Abercrombie and his wife met Jack Wayne Rogers and an unidentified male in at the Travelodge motel in Columbia, Missouri, for gender reassignment surgery—the surgical removal of the penis and scrotum.

"I didn't know his motivation when I went into it. I was under a lot of emotional stress and it seemed like there was no alternative," Madison told the court.

Rogers promised that the procedure would be over in four hours or less. When that time had passed, Rogers was nowhere near done. Complications caused excessive bleeding and Rogers struggled to get the bleeding to stop. Madison survived but the botched operation left her in need of additional surgeries to complete her transformation from male to female. Madison identified herself as the subject of the before and after photographs seized in the search of Rogers' business.

The unnamed assistant of Rogers admitted to participation in similar operations performed on three other men— handing surgical tools to Rogers and taking photographs. He said that Rogers had a standard agreement with all of his "patients." The body parts removed became Rogers' personal property to use as he pleased. Sometimes that meant Rogers would eat them.

The surgical assistant also told authorities that Rogers admitted that one man he operated on died during the procedure. Rogers, he said, kept that man's teeth, and thrown them out the car window as he drove down the road. He did this as a routine part of disposing of a body and obscuring the victim's identity. He added that Rogers often picked up hitchhikers and other transient people and that he was always ready for sexual opportunities—including torture—at any time.

At the conclusion of testimony, the judge said, "Okay. Well, if you want to come forward here by the lectern and I've heard the evidence here," he said, referring to the testimony about surgical castration and cannibalism the state provided in support of their motion of upward departure from the federal sentencing guidelines. "And I'm going to depart upward. And based on the number of images, the extreme nature of the conduct, I can't imagine any more extreme conduct. And, of course, then it was a serious injury that—it's a wonder she didn't die from it. Just a wonder. So, it'll be the judgment of the Court on Counts One through Seven, it'll be the judgment of the Court that the defendant be sentenced to the Bureau of Prisons for a term of thirty years."

Rogers' attorney claimed the sentence was excessive, going far beyond federal sentencing guidelines of 57 to 61 months in prison. She vowed to appeal this violation of Rogers' right to due process.

Meanwhile law enforcement kept digging. They hunted for the evidence they needed to convict Rogers of the crimes they suspected he committed—cannibalism, practicing medicine without a license and the torture and murder of Branson Perry. To their surprise, they discovered there were no federal or state statutes prohibiting cannibalism.

September 2004 was a month of reckoning for Rogers. He received word that the appeal of his child pornography sentence was denied. He also faced a trial on charges of first-degree assault and practicing medicine without a license for the procedure he performed on Madison Abercrombie.

He entered the Boone County courtroom in a zebra-style prison uniform with handcuffs on his wrists and shackles on his ankles. He pled guilty, on the advice of his attorney. He received a sentence of 17 years for the assault and 7 years for the illegal surgery. Both sentences, however, were to be served concurrently with his current 30-year sentence for child pornography.

Law enforcement authorities were gratified that he was behind bars, but still they struggled to build a case against Rogers for murder in the disappearance and presumed death of Branson Perry. They hoped to file charges one day, but feared that the case would never be officially closed.

Of course, the evil heart of Jack Rogers was not touched by the pleas of Branson Perry's family. Not moved by the glares Branson's mother cast in his direction while in the courtroom, he would not divulge any further information about Branson. He would not reveal where he had left the body of a confused young man who should have had a lifetime to find himself.

In 2006, investigators continued to actively pursue the evidence they needed to charge. Rogers for the murder of Branson Perry—and of any other possible homicide victims as well. The results of the forensic analysis of the items seized from Rogers' home, office and vehicles was a closely guarded secret. One day, authorities believed they would have the proof they needed to make a guilty verdict a foregone conclusion.

*   *   *

On March 10, 2004, Branson's father, 49-year-old Bob
Perry, who suffered from dark bouts of depression all of his
life, had a fatal heart attack. He died without knowing the
whereabouts of his oldest son. To Jo Ann Stinnett, Bob Perry
was one more victim of the force of evil known as Jack
Wayne Rogers.

Now the Stinnett clan faced a third nightmare—the lives
of three young people in one generation snuffed out in four
short years. First Wendy, then Branson and now Bobbie Jo—
the wounds cut deep, the pain would not end. The town of
Skidmore clutched one more nightmare to its bosom and
turned its back on the world.

28

In Skidmore, Jo Ann Stinnett said she might have to let a recent family tradition die. She made scrapbooks about every family member who died of an illness, an accident or a murder. She made one for Wendy Gillenwater. She made one for Branson Perry.

But with all of her accumulated grief and pain, she did not know if she could bring herself to start one for Bobbie Jo Stinnett. "They say time heals, and it does," she said, "but time does not make you forget."

In Lyndon, Kansas, in the aftermath of Lisa's arrest, her ex-husband, Carl Boman, told WDAF-TV that Lisa was so wrapped up in her pregnancy story that she needed to come up with a baby to save face. "I believe it drove her, this fact that she didn't want to be proven wrong in this situation. People were looking at her like something wasn't quite right."

* * *

In Deming, New Mexico, the people who knew Lisa and
Carl Boman scratched their heads. Lisa had not ever seemed
to be a violent person. On top of that, she made no secret of
her tubal ligation. She told friends that she regretted having
the procedure because it meant she could not have any more
children, but she did not obsess over having another child.

In Melvern, Kansas, the dazed citizenry struggled to make
sense of it all. The twinkling lights and cheerful Christmas
decorations put up weeks before seemed to mock their sorrow. The joy of the season died an early death and lay buried
beneath their gloom and horror. They performed the rituals
of Christmas with wooden determination, for the sake of the
children. But their hearts were heavy and the days were dark.
    The reason for their community becoming a household
name filled them all with torment. Led by Darrell Schultze,
the Community Pride group that worked year-round to im-
prove the town met informally to tackle the problem. Roger
and Joy Montgomery were active members in the loose-knit
organization, but they were not in attendance at this gathering.
    The group of concerned citizens wanted to rebuild their
image—to let the world know that Melvern was a town full
of good people. Lisa Montgomery was only a solitary aber-
ration, not a common denominator.
    Although none of them knew Bobbie Jo Stinnett, they
ached for her family's loss. They wanted to do something
positive—to assuage their unmerited feelings of guilt and to
reach out a helping hand to a family in another rural community whom they envisioned as kindred spirits.
    They set up a fund for Bobbie Jo's family and hung signs
up and down Melvern's main streets and in the nearby county
seat of Lyndon. The Lyndon State Bank accepted donations
at its branches in both of those towns. They raised a little over
$2,000 in a month and transferred that money up to a bank in
Maitland, Missouri, and into an account in Zeb's name.
    Then they turned their fundraising concerns to finding

money to meet the needs of the children Lisa had left behind. They were sickened by the burden placed on their young shoulders by the thoughtless and despicable actions of their mother. It some ways what these kids had to face in their current circumstances was more difficult and more challenging than if they'd been forced to deal with the death of their mother.

Whistle Stop Café owner Kathy Sage rued the day she ever spoke to the media. Immediately after the arrest of Lisa Montgomery, she was quoted saying: "You read about this stuff. It blows you away when it's here. This stuff is supposed to be in New York City or Los Angeles."

Kathy—along with the whole town of Melvern—was shocked at the massive news coverage the statement received. Melvern rarely made statewide news. Now their every word streaked across the nation and around the world.

Kathy hunkered down as attacks and ridicule for her sound bite rained on her head. Nobody made allowances for the shock of the moment or the inexperience Kathy had with the media. To the world at large, she had spoken, and now she was fair game. Scorn thundered in from journalists in New York and Los Angeles. Worst of all though were the bloggers on the Internet.

One man wrote:

> *This stuff is supposed to be in New York City or Los Angeles.* But strangely happen mostly in the Red States. Just ask Andrea Yates about that. Oh, and most of these pregnant women murders occurred in Red States, too. So, tell me, Ms. Sage, why is it *supposed* to be happening in NYC or LA?
>
> I wasn't going to say anything about this case being an example of Red State pathology, but how insulting can you get, Ms. Sage? This is your crazy neighbor lady, you need to take responsibility in your community for her, don't blame NYC or LA for

her, she wouldn't fit in or be welcome here either. We have [our] own problems and we are just as appalled by your mama-killin'-baby-stealin' crazy as a loon Lisa Montgomery as you are. Possibly more so because, you know what? In a big city somebody might have spotted crazy Lisa and sent in Social Services before she subdued Bobbie Jo Stinnett and sliced her baby out of her still living body. Contrary to popular belief in the Red States, big city people look out for each other. That seems not to have been the case in Skidmore, Missouri or Melvern, Kansas.

A woman in New York added more fuel to the fire:

Ms. Sage, let me assure you, as a New Yorker, as a non-Christian, as a member of a population routinely accused of treating People Not Like Us with contempt: this stuff is **not** supposed to be in New York City or Los Angeles. I assure you, if one of my neighbors came into the Italian deli where I buy my cheese and polenta on a nearly daily basis, with a baby to whom she had just given birth, and we found out three days later that she had murdered a pregnant woman and stolen her child from her body, we would not just be horrified, we would be shocked. We would be in pain for the man who has just lost his wife, the mother of his child; and we would be sickened by the deception practiced on us by a killer. And yes, I'll say it again, we would be shocked, because this stuff, as you put it, is not supposed to be anywhere. Not New York, not Los Angeles. Not Melvern, Kansas or Skidmore, Missouri. Not London, not Paris, not rural China, not Central Africa, not in a packed tenement neighborhood or an isolated farm belt town. This is an abomination no matter where it happened, and your suggestion that it is

less so in my backyard than yours is contemptible.
And I'm sorry, but your shock, while understandable,
does not get you off the hook.

Another blogger lashed out with an attack that encompassed everyone in the Midwest and the South.

Perhaps, like Kathy Sage, Red-Staters are just full
of themselves—and full of something else, too.

The old adage that tragedy brings us all together struck a hollow note. This spirit of brotherhood had been seen many times and in many ways in the past, but at the time of Bobbie Jo's death, the nation was divided and its people divisive. Even a tremendous personal tragedy like this one did not bring out the best in everyone. In the America of 2005, it was easier to find people content to point fingers and scold than it was to find those willing to hold hands and sing "Kum Ba Yah."

29

Law enforcement worked to solidify the case against Lisa Montgomery. They encountered a roadblock when they attempted the forensic analysis of the computer found in the Montgomery home—it was an Apple iMac and their software was created for computers using the Windows operating system.

They knew that important evidence indicating premeditation could be hidden on that hard drive. The case now took a detour to New Zealand.

Daniel Ayers of McCallum Petterson, an accounting firm in Auckland, developed the original Windows-compatible software. The FBI went to the source and asked the New Zealand computer expert to modify the software to work on an iMac.

Ayers was not new to serious crime investigations. He aided law enforcement in abduction and drug trafficking cases in his country and in a murder in Canada. It was his first encounter with a case in the United States, but he plunged in with vigor and determination. Soon authorities had the tool they needed to penetrate any secrets lurking on Lisa's hard drive.

On December 23, Lisa appeared in court again. Under her orange jumpsuit, she wore a dark blue sweatshirt. She sat between her lawyers biting her lips and tugging on her shirt.

When Magistrate Judge Waxse asked her to consent to waive hearings in Kansas, she nodded her head. Waxse asked her to respond out loud. Her voice broke as she said, "Yes"—the only word she uttered during this hearing.

Although her agreement on this point changed the jurisdiction of her case from Kansas City, Kansas, to the Missouri U.S. District Court, Lisa remained incarcerated in the federal penitentiary in Kansas.

On Christmas Day, Patty and Gene Day hosted a dinner party in honor of their great-granddaughter Victoria Jo Stinnett's first Christmas. Grief-stricken family members tried to focus on the joy of Tori Jo, but the memory of her mother hung heavy in the air.

On December 27, at 2:30 P.M., Lisa entered court again—this time in a different state with a new judge—Chief Magistrate John T. Maughmer. She was dressed again in the orange coverall with the dark blue sweatshirt—the outfit accessorized with chains on her hands and feet. Her demeanor was subdued—her voice soft.

Maughmer questioned her to determine whether or not she qualified for a public defender. "Do you have a job?"

"I did," Lisa said.

"How often are you paid?"

"Once every two weeks."

"What type of vehicle do you own?"

"A 1986 Isuzu Trooper."

"How many children do you have?"

"Four."

"Can you read and write?"

"Yes," she said.

After ruling that she was qualified, the judge appointed Anita Burns and David Owen to represent her. The prosecutors informed the court that Nodaway County prosecuting attorney David Baird would be co-counsel and requested that the judge deny bond for Lisa Montgomery. He postponed a decision on that matter until after the New Year. In less than ten minutes, her first appearance in a Missouri courtroom was over.

On January 7, the judge denied the defense request to release their client on bail. He said that there was no set of conditions that could be placed on Montgomery that would be sufficient to ensure the safety of others.

30

The courts granted custody of Lisa's four children to Carl. Kevin wanted them all to stay with him. Three of the children chose to live with their biological father. The oldest, Desiree, however, elected to stay with Kevin in Melvern to finish her senior year in high school. She continued managing the basketball team and getting good grades. The student body had not ostracized her as she had feared, but embraced her as a victim and a friend. After the school year ended, she still remained in Melvern and—with the community's financial help—attended college classes in Emporia.

Desiree went to see her mother in prison as often as she could, but a suicide watch was in place and that often prohibited Lisa from having any visitors. Visits with Lisa helped her to cope with the new reality of her life.

Kevin, though, was lost. He did not cope well at all. He found it very difficult to accept the reality of the woman he married. He avoided talking whenever possible and carried the demeanor of a widower—grieving the loss of a woman he thought he knew and the illusion of a daughter who existed only in his heart.

The townspeople provided as much emotional support and encouragement as they could, too—to both Desiree and Kevin. The ceaseless baying of the media and the unending train of curiosity seekers drove Kevin from his home and away from the rooms filled with memories of the Lisa he thought he knew. In January, he and Desiree moved into the modest home of Roger and Joy just blocks away from downtown Melvern.

Kevin kept paying the rent on the farmhouse through April as if that act would transform the last few months into nothing but a dreadful nightmare and allow him to return to the life he knew before December 16. Without that miracle, he could not bear to walk through the door of his former home on South Adams Road. Roger and Joy took charge of cleaning up and clearing the house before turning the key back to Isabel Phelon.

Zeb Stinnett was numb, too. With quiet dignity, he accepted awkward expressions of sorrow and gifts of sympathy. On Bobbie Jo's website, he watched emails that once sent wishes for the safe return of his baby morph into condolences and promises of prayer. Zeb withdrew from the public eye.

The second week of January, the grand jury convened in Kansas City, Missouri. The prosecutor alleged that Lisa Montgomery killed Bobbie Jo Stinnett in "a heinous, cruel and depraved manner" and that the murder included torture and physical abuse. Thirty-two jurors and three judges listened to the testimony about the crime. When Sheriff Espey took the stand, his description of the attack on Bobbie Jo caused six jurors to cry out loud.

Espy turned to a judge, questioning the necessity for his graphic recounting of the events on Elm Street.

A judge said, "You've got to tell it like it is."

Espey continued his gruesome tale of strangulation and

brutal amateur surgery accompanied by a backup chorus of sobs. The only other witness at the hearing was Special Agent Kurt Lipanovich from the FBI.

U.S. Attorney Todd Graves focused the jurors' attention on the definitions in their manual. " 'Heinous,' " he read out loud, "means extremely wicked or shockingly evil, where the killing was accompanied by such additional acts of torture or serious physical abuse of the victim as to set it apart from other killings.

" 'Cruel' means that the defendant relished the killing or showed indifference to the suffering of the victim, as evidenced by torture or serious physical abuse of the victim. 'Depraved' means that the defendant relished the killing or showed indifference to the suffering to the victim, as evidenced by torture or serious physical abuse of the victim.

" 'Torture,' " he continued, "means the victim must have been conscious of the abuse at the time it was inflicted, and the defendant must have specifically intended to inflict severe mental or physical pain or suffering on the victim, in addition to the killing of the victim." He argued that torture could apply in this case, since Bobbie Jo may still have been alive when Lisa cut the baby out of her body.

The grand jury returned an indictment charging that Lisa Montgomery a/k/a Darlene Fischer "willfully and unlawfully kidnapped, abducted, carried away, and held Victoria Jo Stinnett, and willfully transported Victoria Jo Stinnett in interstate commerce from Skidmore, Missouri, across the state line to Melvern, Kansas, the actions of the defendant resulting in the death of Bobbie Jo Stinnett."

The indictment went on to cite eleven special findings including "participation in an act that constituted a reckless disregard for human life," the death and injury of Bobbie Jo Stinnett in the commission of another crime, the "especially heinous, cruel and depraved manner" of that killing, the existence of "substantial planning and premeditation," and the vulnerability of both of the victims—one for her young age, the other for her pregnancy.

The new indictment replaced the criminal complaint originally filed with U.S. Magistrate Judge Sarah Hayes on December 17 by FBI Special Agent Craig Arnold to incarcerate Lisa. The grand jury ruling now provided the authorization to keep Lisa behind bars.

"The wording of this indictment," Graves said, "lays the groundwork for the pursuit of the death penalty." The final decision of that matter was not up to the local federal prosecutor's office, though. "It'll take months to go through that process. That is a decision that will be made by the Department of Justice as a whole, and at the highest level of the Department of Justice." The final approval of that decision required the signature of no one less than the Attorney General of the United States. "The nature of these charging documents," Graves said, "is to protect our opportunity and our option to seek the death penalty."

When asked about the possibility of charges being filed against Kevin Montgomery, Graves said, "The investigation is ongoing. I do not anticipate any other charges against this defendant, but I will not rule out charges against other potential defendants."

Swarmed by the media, a weary Judy Shaughnessy did not offer any excuses for her daughter's behavior or argue in defense of her innocence. She said, "All her lies were catching up to her. I think the desperation got to her. I did not have any sense she could murder someone. I thought she could maybe steal or buy a child—but not kill to get one."

Bobbie Jo's mother, Becky Harper, did not try to hide the seething anger and intense loathing she had for Lisa Montgomery. When she spoke to reporters, she said, "I hope she gets the death penalty. I don't want to have to pay for her to be in jail."

31

On January 20, 2005, Lisa Montgomery returned to court for her formal indictment on federal charges that made her eligible for the death penalty. The jingle of the chains at her wrists and ankles preceded her into the chamber.

Her face was flat, slack and empty. Any small flicker betraying her underlying emotional turmoil disappeared as quickly as it arrived. She spoke not a word during her fifteen-minute hearing. Her public defender entered her pleas of not guilty to U.S. Chief Magistrate John Maughmer.

"Has the United States made any judgment as to whether it will seek certification of the death penalty?" Maughmer asked the prosecution.

"The investigation in this case is ongoing," Graves said. "The final determination will be made by the attorney general. But that is the direction that we are going, and that is our present inclination."

The judge indicated that the possibility of a death penalty case required that he appoint a third attorney for the defense of Lisa Montgomery. A tentative trial date was set for March 14, 2006.

On February 9, attorneys for the defense and the prosecution met for a scheduling conference in Todd Graves' office. The state presented a number of items, including the incriminating statements made by the defendant. Lisa's lawyers admitted their client did not have an alibi, but would instead rely on the defense of general denial—in other words, she would claim she did not do it.

They laid out the basic facts accepted by both sides—including that there was no electronic surveillance and the defendant had no prior criminal record. They reached agreement on when they were required to share particular documents and evidence, on when motions were due in court and regarding what background information needed to be revealed about both lay and expert witnesses. This meeting paved the way for a smooth formal procedure before the judge on February 25. The court proposed that the trial would commence on April 24, 2006. The defense countered with a request for an August trial. They were overruled and the calendar was set for April.

Also at that hearing, the defense informed the court that they did not intend to argue that their client was incompetent to stand trial or help in her own defense. They did, however, reserve the right to prepare a defense based on insanity or on diminished mental responsibility.

Many lawyers, forensic psychologists and other court observers felt that it was the only defense with any hope of success. It was an approach taken by only one percent of all defendants in criminal court. The likelihood of its working had diminished to a great extent since John Hinckley was found not guilty by reason of insanity in his trial for the shooting of President Reagan. Potential jurors across the country were hardened by that verdict and defense attorneys were reluctant to use it again.

Current federal law stated that the pursuit of an insanity

defense was appropriate if the "defendant as a result of severe mental disease or defect was unable to appreciate the nature and quality or the wrongfulness of his acts."

Under that definition, the defense had grounds to pursue the plea. The first and most obvious avenue was that Lisa had faked pregnancies on five separate occasions—in at least one, her stomach grew as hard and large as that of a genuine expectant mother. Second was the gruesome nature of the crime. Although the state's position was that this justified seeking the death penalty, the defense could argue with ease that it proved mental instability in their otherwise law-abiding client. Third was premeditation. Once again, this was an area that the state would argue was a reason to impose the ultimate penalty. Lisa's attorneys, on the other hand, could use it to demonstrate Lisa's delusional thinking.

A plea of insanity was a tool Lisa's public defenders could pull out of their belts at any point—as a pre-trial motion or in the acquittal phase or the punishment phase of the trial. Success before the commencement of the trial could result in the judge throwing out Lisa's confession. If that occurred, it could impact the outcome of the trial. It is the duty of a jury to determine the facts of the case and to decide if they fit the definition of the charged crime. In doing so, they can consider only the pieces of evidence that the judge deemed legally admissible.

There was good news, though, for those who feared that a potentially dangerous Lisa would be judged insane and be put out on the streets again. A recent study by the American Psychiatric Association demonstrated that defendants found not guilty on these grounds spent as much or more time in custody as those who are convicted and sent to prison.

In the first week of February, Attorney General John Ashcroft prepared to step down from his office and turn the reins of the Justice Department over to his replacement, Alberto Gonzales. He addressed the Heritage Foundation focusing on the importance of the Patriot Act.

He credited that act with facilitating the quick arrest of Lisa Montgomery and the successful recovery of Victoria Jo Stinnett. Without the act, he said, authorities could not have had the instantaneous access to the email on Bobbie Jo's computer that led them to the perpetrator in record time. The safe return of the abducted infant he said was "a final act of grace in a sad, savage drama."

Later that week, the United States Senate confirmed the appointment of Alberto Gonzales. He now bore the responsibility for the Department of Justice, including the decision on whether or not to seek the death penalty for Lisa Montgomery.

At Leavenworth Detention Center, Lisa was removed from suicide watch. She was out of her cell on recreation time when a jailer searched her space. In it, he found a letter indicating that she was stockpiling medications for a suicide attempt.

Another search ensued and the hidden prescription drugs were recovered. Also seized from her cell were correspondence and other documents, including a letter to her daughter Desiree that had a "strong suicidal theme." The U.S. Marshall's Office turned all those papers over to Judge Maughmer. Anita Burns, assistant public defender, argued successfully that some of the documents should be withheld from the prosecution, since they fell under attorney–client privilege.

But Burns could not conceal the medications or prevent the inevitable outcome of their discovery. A psychiatrist ordered Lisa back on suicide watch. She was placed in a private cell in the medical unit. The prison issued her a "suicide gown" and a "suicide blanket"—both made of a tough, tear-resistant fabric that made it difficult, if not impossible, to use in the construction of a noose. All of Lisa's belongings were removed from her possession and corrections officers were assigned to watch her at all times. After being moved, Lisa cried for forty-five minutes without stopping.

As Lisa languished behind bars, her family members paid for her sins. Patty had a part-time job as an on-site manager for an apartment complex. A perk of that position was the apartment where she lived with her family.

According to Judy, a pregnant woman in the complex complained about Patty's presence there. She was worried that Patty's "crazy sister" would visit and take her baby. Patty lost her job and was evicted from her home.

Judy said that she received many threatening phone calls. She developed a habit of traveling to a different town to do her shopping to avoid the people who knew her and her family. Now raising Teddy's little boy Justin, she was determined, she said, "to keep it together for my grandson."

32

While the homicide committed by Lisa Montgomery tore apart the lives of her own family and kept her lawyers busy fighting for her life, another woman obsessed and fantasized about pregnancy. But when she attacked a pregnant woman, the outcome was remarkably different.

Katie Smith grew up in Independence, Kentucky. Some childhood friends remember her as a spirited, fun-loving girl. Her family, however, remembered her panic attacks, which began at an early age. They knew of the hypochondria that led her to believe that she suffered from an ever-changing series of medical problems ranging from fibromyalgia to Crohn's disease. In junior high school she insisted she was pregnant when she was not. They tried to get help for Katie—tried to liberate her from her delusions and obsessions—but nothing seemed to help.

When Katie was 17 years old, she claimed she had sex with a boyfriend. In the middle of the act, she saw her father's face supplanted over her lover's. At that moment, she said, suppressed and repressed memories of childhood sexual abuse emerged. The young man, denied any sexual activity with Katie. In fact, he even denied being her boyfriend at any time.

Katie filed a criminal complaint against her father, Timothy Smith, alleging that he'd molested her from the time she was 7 years old until she was 12. He denied her accusations. Despite his protestations of innocence, he was convicted of first-degree sodomy and sentenced to 20 years in an eastern Kentucky state prison.

After a family funeral in April 2004, Katie told a cousin, "I've had two miscarriages in the past year and the second time, it was twins I buried." She carried a sonogram image of the twins she claimed to have lost and showed it to many friends. Katie also insinuated that when she claimed sexual abuse at the hands of her father, she made these accusations for one self-serving reason—she wanted to get him out of the house.

In the summer of 2004, Katie claimed she was expecting again as she moved out of her apartment in Wallace Woods. A neighbor there said she was wearing maternity clothing and appeared to be pregnant. Among the items she packed up for the move were a baby seat and books on parenting and baby care.

Katie moved into another apartment located in Fort Mitchell. She set up a nursery in one room as soon as she arrived. She stocked it with baby furniture, infant's clothing, diapers and formula. She also added surgical equipment including an umbilical clamp, hemostats, scissors, latex gloves and absorbent pads.

She wore an outfit padded to make her appear pregnant every time she left her house or entertained a visitor at home. She kept changing her delivery date—pushing it forward in time.

She showed off a laparoscopy scar to family and friends—telling them that she got the scar when she had a caesarean section the year before. She worked as a nanny for an ophthalmologist in the fall of 2004. She was fired when her employer realized that she faked her pregnancy, and worried that she was too unstable to be entrusted with the care of the children.

As the year came to an end, Katie remained unemployed and life was becoming more difficult. She was about to be evicted from her apartment for failure to pay rent. She told her landlord that she couldn't throw her out because she was pregnant with a Lakeside Park police officer's baby.

On February 10, Katie called 26-year-old Sarah Brady, a 9-month-pregnant woman whose name she found on the Babies R Us gift registry. Katie introduced herself as Sarah Brodie. She laughingly told Sarah about the mix-up in the similarity in their names that resulted in her receiving a delivery that belonged to the unsuspecting Brady.

Sarah stopped by and picked up the package. The women chatted about their pregnancies. Katie said she was past due. Sarah empathized with her—her due date had been a week before on February 3.

Katie called again. She had another of Sarah's gifts, she said. She told Sarah that she had to pick it up on February 11. After making these arrangements, Katie told her family that her baby was due that day.

Sarah dropped by for the pickup and Katie invited her in to see the nursery. On her way to that room, Sarah saw papers with the name of Katie Smith written on them—and the address matched this apartment. A warning flashed in her head—something wasn't right here. She walked ahead of Katie and into the baby's room. Sarah heard the click of a locking door.

"I have to leave now," Sarah said. "I have to pick my son up at school." Katie begged her not to leave, but Sarah pushed her way to the door, unlocked it and headed for the exit.

Katie's pleas slowed down Sarah's escape. She paused to allow Katie to give her a hug. Katie thanked Sarah for her kindness and her time. Then Katie reached into her pocket and pulled out a folding knife with a four-inch blade. "If you leave, I'll kill you," Katie shrieked.

Katie pulled the knife back over her head and slashed down at Sarah. Sarah backed up and Katie slashed at her again. Sarah stumbled out through the apartment door. Katie grabbed her by the hair and dragged her back inside.

Sarah grabbed a heavy ashtray and slammed it into the side of Katie's head. Katie dropped the knife. Sarah scrambled after it. They fought for control of the weapon. Then it was in Sarah's hand.

Sarah stabbed Katie in the right shoulder blade. All she could think of was saving her baby and saving her own life. She stabbed Katie in her left shoulder. Still Katie struggled to reclaim the knife. Katie bit. She scratched. She clawed at Sarah like a cornered animal.

Sarah stabbed Katie again. This time, the blade went into Katie's chest. It passed through skin, fat and muscles until it reached a major blood vessel, the superior vena cava. That injury was mortal—the bleeding would not stop.

Still clutching the knife, Sarah staggered out of the apartment building and toward Dixie Highway. Her clothes were covered in blood. She waved the knife in the air trying to flag down someone for help. She collapsed in the grass on the side of the road. Her appearance scared the motorists on the crowded highway more than it compelled them to come to her aid. But one driver did call and report the unusual circumstances.

Inside the apartment, Katie pulled off the padding that made her appear pregnant. She grabbed the phone and punched in 9-1-1. She talked to dispatchers until extreme blood loss caused her to lose consciousness.

Six police cars and four ambulances screeched to a stop in front of the apartment building, their sirens resonating in the

air. The lights continued flashing as police and paramedics
fanned out to care for the two injured women. Other tenants
thought Katie was having her baby.

In one ambulance, Sarah was rushed to the hospital, where
she was treated for bites and stab wounds on her hands and
arms and then released. Katie arrived in another ambulance.
She was declared dead on arrival—she lost too much blood.
When Katie's family members arrived at the hospital, their
first question was: "How's the baby?"

However, the autopsy performed on Katie Smith uncovered her ruse. Katie Smith was not pregnant. In fact, she had
never been pregnant in her life.

Sarah had a professional caesarean section at St. Elizabeth
Medical Center on February 16. Her daughter, McKaila Grace
Hutton, weighed seven pounds and four ounces.

Authorities verified Sarah's version of the events the afternoon of the attack and believed her claims of self-defense
against a woman determined to kill her and steal her baby.
No charges were filed against Sarah Brady.

The story of the incident made an impact in the courts
just the same. It drew the attention of the Kentucky Innocence Project, who looked into the conviction of Katie's father. They concluded that Katie's history of deception and
the dubious reliability of recovered memory called Timothy
Smith's verdict into question.

It also captured the imagination of attorney Patrick Lamb
of a law firm in Chicago. He was convinced of Smith's innocence in the sexual abuse accusations. He offered the *pro
bono* services of his firm to the incarcerated man. Smith accepted his offer.

Lamb filed a brief requesting an evidentiary hearing on
behalf of their new client. The filing included affidavits
from Katie's two sisters and one of her cousins, attesting
that they believed Katie's accusations about her father
were false. Other affidavits included statements from expert witnesses that cast doubt on the credibility of recovered memory.

*   *   *

In Skidmore, Missouri, they rejoiced at Sarah Brady's survival. They closed their eyes and imagined different headlines in last December's newspapers—headlines that marveled at Bobbie Jo Stinnett's ability to fend off her attacker—headlines that announced the funeral of Lisa Montgomery.

33

Zeb Stinnett emerged from his self-imposed exile in mid-April and issued a statement to the public:

Over the past four months, I am sure I have been a source of frustration to the many reporters who have requested interviews. This is not because of any ill will toward the media. To be honest, I respect the hard work reporters do, and I will always be deeply grateful for their crucial role in returning my daughter to me. With that said, right now my family is seeking as much normalcy as possible. Anyone who knows me will tell you that talking is not my favorite pastime. I am quiet even among family and friends, so you can imagine how I feel about appearing on TV or in newspaper articles.

For the foreseeable future, I, as well as the members of my family, won't be available to the news media. I respectfully ask that all inquiries be directed to my spokesman, Dan Madden. I thank you for your cooperation.

To the many people who have prayed for our family, who have sent letters and emails and who have generously given their time and money to help give Victoria Jo a better future, I hope my public silence is not misinterpreted as ingratitude. My words could never be enough to convey what it has meant to our family. We are humbled and awed by the kindness that has flooded into our lives. To see such goodness in the wake of what happened gave us strength to persevere. I assure you that Victoria will be told about all of you and, like us, I know she will be touched deeply by your kindness.

Speaking of Victoria, she is four months old and beautiful. She has three great loves right now— eating, sleeping and smiling. Believe it or not, the 5-pound, 11-ounce baby I held in a Kansas hospital last December now weighs 15 pounds, 8 ounces—most of it cheeks.

Our family is strong. We have stuck together and thanks to the help of my mother-in-law Becky, my mother Patty, and many other relatives and close friends, Victoria is deeply loved and well cared for.

I must express my thanks to many people. My regret is that there are so many that we will never be able to personally thank each person who has touched our lives in the past months.

First of all, we want to thank Nodaway County Sheriff Ben Espey and his staff for their quick work and persistence in getting the Amber Alert started. Sam Graves, who intervened on Tori Jo's behalf; David Merrill and the Missouri Highway Patrol; Randy Strong of Maryville Public Safety; the Northwest Missouri Major Case Squad; the FBI; and Todd Graves and Matthew Whitworth of the U.S. Attorney's Office.

We would also like to express our support for the "Tori Jo's Loophole" bill that would amend the Amber Alert system.

We are deeply grateful to Dr. Siglinger and the administrators and staff of Stormont-Vail HealthCare in Topeka, who cared for Victoria in those first few days, and to the responding team of Nodaway County Ambulance and the ER doctors and staff at St. Francis Hospital who tried to save Bobbie Jo.

A special thank you to the people of northwest Missouri, especially our friends and family, the pastors and members of our churches, our employers and co-workers at Kawasaki Motors and Sumy Oil Company, and Richard Dowden and the people at Price Funeral Home. We also give special thanks to the people at S&M NuTec, the makers of Little Greenies dog treats, who established a $15,000 education trust fund for Tori Jo, the Mead and Johnson Company who generously donated a year's supply of formula, the Dollar General Store of Maryville, which donated a year's supply of diapers and baby supplies, and to the JC Penny Outlet of Maryville for the gift of a changing table and crib set.

To the fifth-grade class at Nodaway-Holt Elementary School and the sixth-grade class at Savannah Middle School, your colorful cards and letters brightened some pretty dark days.

I personally have received hundreds of cards, letters and e-mails from around the world. I am reading each and every one. There is no way to thank each person who has reached out to us, but I hope you all know that you have given us a priceless gift.

Our thanks go to United Missouri Bank and Bank Midwest who established funds for Victoria and to the countless people who have made donations. We are humbled by your generosity.

With the grace of God, and the good will of so

> *many people, we will emerge from this stronger and*
> *more appreciative of His many blessings.*
>
> *Please continue to pray for us and for all families*
> *who have suffered from violence. We can feel your*
> *prayers.*

Every year, the U.S. Department of Justice and the National
Center for Missing and Exploited Children selected six cases
across the country for special recognition. Sheriff Espey received notification that one of those cases for 2004 was the
safe recovery of Victoria Jo Stinnett.

At 4 A.M. on Tuesday, May 17, the sheriff and a team of
officers and three Nodaway County Sheriff's Department
dispatchers—Marla Finney, Melissa Wallace, Lindsey Stiens
and Joni Sherman—boarded an airplane bound for Washington, D.C. The next morning, they were honored at a congres-
sional breakfast meeting. United States Representative Sam
Graves of northwest Missouri presented the 2005 National
Missing Children's Award. John Walsh, host of *America's
Most Wanted*, bestowed the Officer of the Year award on the
group from Missouri.

After that ceremony, they were free until Friday. They
spent the time sightseeing at as many Washington, D.C.,
landmarks as possible. The Smithsonian National Air and
Space Museum was a big hit. The memorials to fallen heroes
humbled them with a reminder of the sacrifices made by the
men and women of the military throughout the nation's history. On May 20, they headed to the Department of Justice
for an awards banquet for them and twenty other members
of law enforcement from across the nation.

The team who rescued Victoria Jo Stinnett received the
Officers of the Year award. Attorney General Alberto Gonzales passed out the National Missing Children's Law Enforcement Awards to the remaining officers.

Four officers from the Philadelphia Police Department
received an award for the recovery of 10-day-old Delimar
Vera. Although Delimar was presumed to have perished in

the fire that destroyed her home, law enforcement found her in the care of the woman who set the fire to cover up the abduction.

Two officers from the Linn County Sheriff's Office in Albany, Oregon, were honored for the recovery of 11-year-old Tanner Kahn after his mother's boyfriend kidnapped him from a bus stop. An officer from the Midwest City Police Department in Oklahoma received his award for dismantling a child sex ring.

Seven officers from New Jersey and two from Florida were recognized for the multistate operation that shut down a child pornography enterprise. The final case, the capture of three men involved in a child sex and pornography ring, earned the award for a team of four out of North Carolina.

Alberto Gonzales acknowledged the efforts of others as well. Trucker Charles Cogburn of Russellville, Arkansas, received the Amber Alert Citizen Award. He paid attention and responded to the alert when he spotted 17-year-old Shauna Leigh of Plano, Texas, in the vehicle of her abductor. His call led to the apprehension of the suspect and the safe release of the victim.

Corporate awards were given to Honeywell and Radio Shack for their child safety programs. And the National Missing Children's Day art contest winner was fifth-grader Dana Server from Alimitos Elementary School in San Jose, California.

The next day the folks from northwest Missouri flew back home. One more trip to D.C. was in the works, but this time Espey was told that only five officers could be in the group. With all the people who had helped in the effort, picking a handful was a difficult decision. He selected as representative a group of investigators as he could: Corporal Jeffrey Owen and Sergeant Dave Merrill of the Missouri Highway Patrol, Investigator Randy Strong of the Maryville Department of Public Safety and FBI Special Agent Kurt Lipanovich.

Three days later, these five officers were on a plane again.

On the afternoon of May 25—National Missing Children's Day—they were admitted into the White House.

After passing through security, staffers ushered the thirty recipients to be honored that day into the briefing room. The presidential aides walked them through the upcoming presentation, explaining what the President would say and where they should stand.

The five honorees in the Skidmore case were the last group to leave the staging area and enter the Oval Office. Attorney General Albert Gonzales gave a summary of the accomplishments of the group to the President and introduced each of the men. One by one, Bush shook their hands and expressed his appreciation for their hard work to recover the baby. He said he'd followed the story on the news.

Then President Bush addressed the full group. He talked about items of historical significance in the Oval Office like the desk that was the room's focal point. He drew their attention to the painting of a springtime bounty of bluebonnets that stretched across a Texas Hill Country landscape—*Near San Antonio* by Julian Onderdunk, on loan from the San Antonio Museum of Art. He pointed to the left of his desk to a painting of men on horseback—*Charge to Keep* by William Koerner. This piece of art had particular significance to the President because he had borrowed it from a personal friend.

He directed his audience to the paintings beside the fireplace. On the right was *Rio Grande* by Tom Lea, a cactus-strewn desert scene from the El Paso Museum of Art. On the left were two smaller pieces on loan from the Witte Museum: *Chili Queens at the Alamo*, a rendering of the former tradition of chili stand vendors, and *Cactus Flowers,* which glowed with the yellow and orange-red blooms of the Prickly Pear. The other two paintings in the Oval Office were historical national treasures: portraits of George Washington and Abraham Lincoln.

Then Bush said, "I'm going to have to boot y'all out of here now, 'cause I have work to do." He thanked them again for their service and sent them on their way.

The Missouri team was dazzled by their visit to the White House. Strong said that the Oval Office seemed smaller than what he thought it would be, but was still very grand. "The historical impact of what happened in that room, the decisions made there and the people who passed through there and made those decisions was overwhelming. I felt as if I was in the center of the free world and it was awesome."

Sheriff Espey added: "Going into the Oval Office and shaking George Bush's hand—I don't have any words for it. It's about as high an honor as you can get."

The prosecution enlisted the services of a forensic psychiatrist, Dr. Park Dietz in May. Dietz's reputation had been clouded by the false statements he made in the first trial of Andrea Yates, the Houston area woman who drowned her five children. Nonetheless, prosecutors still valued his expertise in the courtroom.

For the first time in June 2005, Guidance Software, a forensic technology firm, distributed the annual Timothy Fidel Memorial Award. Timothy Fidel was a pioneer in digital forensics, a Special Agent with the United States Secret Service and the Environmental Protection Agency's Criminal Investigation Division. He passed away on October 29, 2004. The judges who selected the honoree made their decision based on the use of best practices, industry standards or other innovative techniques in a computer forensic investigation; the complexity or notoriety of the case; and the financial, procedural, organizational or societal impact of the investigation.

Two groups of investigators were honored for work performed in 2004. The Modesto, California, law enforcement officials who worked on the Laci Peterson investigation and the three forensic computer professionals who aided in the recovery of Victoria Jo Stinnett—Corporal Jeff Owen of the Missouri Highway Patrol, Mark Johnson of the United States Attorney's Office and Curtis Howard of the St. Joseph Police Department. Each received the recognition and a

$2,500 cash award. The northwest Missouri team donated their gift to the Special Olympics of Missouri.

In October 2005, Judy Clarke, an attorney and national death penalty opponent filed paperwork in federal court requesting that she be added to the defense team despite the fact that the attorney general had not yet approved the pursuit of a death sentence—a decision that was supposed to be delivered to the court in mid-September.

Clarke had never cringed from the defense of the criminals that America loved to loathe. Through plea agreements and courtroom rhetoric, she spared a number of them from Death Row. That number included Susan Smith, the South Carolina mother convicted of drowning her two young sons in her car; the bomber of Olympic Park and an abortion clinic, Eric Rudolph; and Unabomber Ted Kaczynski. Clarke, a federal public defender in California, was once described by a colleague as a "one-woman dream team."

The court accepted her petition, creating a defense team for Lisa Montgomery consisting of three attorneys and three mitigation specialists. On the prosecution side, the government had four lawyers led by U.S. Attorney Todd Graves.

In the midst of Lisa Montgomery's legal waltz, another pregnant woman danced with death at the hands of yet another desperate female attacker. Valerie Oskin was born in Colorado Springs, Colorado, grew up in Texas and moved to Pennsylvania when she graduated from high school.

She moved from run-down apartments to seedy trailer park neighborhoods. She suffered through serial abusive relationships. She eked out a living on the low pay of one nurses' aide job after another. Her son Brandon was born in August 1998.

In February 2005, a pregnant Valerie rented a white-and-blue mobile home in a weary trailer park near Ford City, Pennsylvania. Her next-door neighbors were Peggy Jo Conner, her three children, and Thomas "Cowboy" Wilks from Texas. Peggy Jo introduced him as her husband.

Peggy Jo, too, had a hardscrabble life. She was a high school drop-out who married at the age of 18 in August 1985. Her spouse was John Harvey, the 22-year-old building manager in the apartment complex where she lived with her mother.

In 1990, the couple had a daughter, Amanda. Soon after her birth, they separated, but did not divorce. Peggy Jo met James Conner in a bar and he fathered her second child, Jason, born nineteen months after Amanda. In 1993, Peggy Jo and James had a daughter, Kaylie.

Peggy Jo finally got a divorce from John Harvey in 1995. She married James Conner in 1997 but left him when she met Cowboy Wilks in May 2004. Cowboy moved in with her and her three children that summer.

In 2005, Peggy Jo was bragging about her pregnancy and walking with a waddle—one hand resting on her stomach, the other pressing into her lower back. She presented a sonogram to Cowboy and told him that it was their baby. In reality, what she gave him was a 1993 image of her third child Kaylie. But Cowboy believed it was his child and hung the sonogram up on the wall of their trailer for everyone to see.

Cowboy's passion for Peggy Jo was waning, but he loved babies—he played with a friend's infant son every chance he had. Now, he believed he had a baby on the way. He got busy building a room onto their mobile home for the baby's nursery. Peggy Jo haunted yard sales, picking up an assortment of baby clothing, supplies and furniture, including a bassinet, a crib and a baby swing.

Meanwhile, next-door neighbor Valerie Oskin, who really was pregnant, was denying the reality of her condition to everyone who asked. By summer of 2005, her pregnancy was too obvious to avoid. She accepted the reality and made arrangements to give the child up for adoption. She did not feel she would be able to raise a second child.

Valerie and Peggy Jo spent a lot of time talking about their pregnancies, waddling between each other's trailers and becoming fast friends. On Tuesday, October 11, Peggy Jo dropped in on Valerie again.

Valerie had no reason to suspect that it was anything but a typical neighborly visit. She had no reason to fear turning her back on Peggy Jo. But when she did, Peggy Jo slammed a baseball bat into the back of her head.

Peggy Jo led a dazed Valerie and her 7-year-old son Brandon from the trailer out to her blue Dodge Dynasty. Landlord Betty Theverin saw the trio and expressed her concern about the condition of the bloodied Valerie.

"Don't worry. I'll take care of it," Peggy Jo said.

"You need to get her to a hospital," Betty urged.

"That's where we're going."

Instead, Peggy Jo drove to a family member's home and dropped Brandon off while an unconscious Valerie lay in the backseat of the Dodge. Peggy Jo drove fifteen miles out to a lonely, wooded area off Route 1037. She pulled to the side of the road and dragged Valerie out and laid her on the ground.

Seventeen-year-old Adam Silvis was out riding on his ATV in that same secluded area. He approached Peggy Jo's blue Dynasty. He spotted a bundle of something beside it and thought, at first, that the driver was dumping trash. As he got closer, Peggy Jo ran out in front of the vehicle and said, "Everything's fine here."

"Okay," Adam said.

"I'm just looking for a place to hunt," she said.

Adam was troubled—something did not seem right. He masked his concern and said, "I'm just going back to check my hunting stand."

Once the sound of the ATV faded into the distance, Peggy Jo took a razor knife and started an incision in Valerie's belly. Adam, though, was worried and turned around after a short distance and returned to where the car was parked.

This time, Adam recognized the bundle beside the road as a body covered in blood—blood on her head, blood on her stomach. Peggy Jo knelt on the ground right next to the body—Adam knew there could not be an innocent explanation for that. As he sped off toward home, Peggy Jo waved and smiled.

She returned to her unholy mission when the sound of his engine dimmed again. Carefully, she followed the line of Valerie's old caesarean scar like a template. She stopped when the incision was seven inches long.

The return of Adam and his father interrupted her again. Adam's dad was shocked—his son had not exaggerated or imagined things. Adam's unbelievable story was very real. He called the police. Spooked by their visit, Peggy Jo fled the scene.

When authorities arrived, bloodied towels and blankets littered the ground around Valerie. She appeared close to death. They radioed for a helicopter and Valerie was airlifted to Allegheny General Hospital in Pittsburgh. After an emergency caesarean, mother and baby were moved into the hospital's trauma care unit.

Police arrested Peggy Jo Conner. In her Dodge Dynasty, they recovered a pair of scissors, a bulb syringe, a razor knife, shoelaces and a hemostat. Peggy Jo faced charges of attempted homicide, aggravated assault and aggravated assault of an unborn child. The prosecutors sought the same level of sentencing as they would for first-degree murder.

Investigators questioned Cowboy Wilks. He wore a wedding band and said he was Peggy Jo's husband. When pressed, he admitted that they were not legally wed, but "in my heart, we're married," he said.

He insisted that Peggy Jo was pregnant—telling officers he'd seen the sonogram and felt the baby kick. He denied the possibility that Peggy Jo could have attacked Valerie. In fact, he was angry that the accusation was ever made.

When the media asked him about Peggy Jo's assault of Valerie, he said, "No, that's totally a lie. I'll tell everybody right now, that's a lie." He went on to talk about the close friendship between the two women—how Peggy Jo shared her experiences with childbirth with their neighbor—and said that Peggy Jo was a loving mother of three children.

"They won't let me talk to her. They won't let me see her. Once I talk to her, I'll know what's going on." He insisted again that it was impossible that Peggy Jo committed this crime.

Once Thomas was permitted to see Peggy Jo, he went to see her every day that visitation was allowed at the Armstrong County Jail. He made sure to park his van within the view of Peggy Jo's second-floor cell so that she could see him coming and going. He still proclaimed his undying love.

Adam Silvis had trouble sleeping for weeks after he stumbled on the scene. Every time he closed his eyes, he saw the bloody visions he wanted to forget. Valerie's 7-year-old son Brandon dealt with his emotional scars by sleeping through the better part of every day.

On December 14, 2005, Peggy Jo Conner appeared before Judge Joseph A. Nickleach and pled not guilty on all charges.

Valerie's baby—born one month premature—was doing well despite all the obstacles. Valerie Oskin's healing was slow but steady. Her physical recovery was expected—her emotional recovery uncertain.

34

In the early afternoon of November 16, U.S. Attorney Todd Graves submitted the *Notice of Intent to Seek the Death Penalty* to the U.S. District Court for the Western District of Missouri proclaiming that ". . . the government believes a sentence of death is justified, and the government will seek a sentence of death." His grounds in his filing detailed the heinous nature of the crime and included the allegation that "Lisa M. Montgomery committed the offense after substantial planning and premeditation to cause the death of a person" and that "Bobbie Jo Stinnett, the murder victim, was particularly vulnerable due to her infirmity, that is, at the time of her death Bobbie Jo Stinnett was eight months pregnant." Also enclosed was a letter from Attorney General Alberto Gonzales giving his approval dated the week before the filing. No plea agreement to spare Montgomery from possible execution could be reached without the approval of the attorney general.

On the same day, Graves also announced another death penalty decision. Missouri resident John Phillip Street would also face the possibility of the ultimate punishment. Street was charged with the 1998 death of Doug Wells of Independence, Missouri. Prosecutors claimed Street had killed Wells to prevent him from cooperating with federal agents investigating a methamphetamine ring.

In his press release, Graves pointed out that there are thirty-six prisoners currently under sentence of death in the federal system, including four from the Western District of Missouri. He said, "As these numbers indicate, we intend to prosecute federal defendants to the full extent of the law, and will not shy away from seeking the ultimate penalty for the ultimate crime. Our decision to seek the death penalty in each of these cases is made with careful deliberation so that justice is served."

Todd Graves' brother, U.S. Representative Sam Graves, had not just talked about fixing the Amber Alert communications network, he had taken action. On the same day he was sworn in to serve his third term—January 4, 2005—he filed the "Tory Jo's Loophole" bill in the House of Representatives. Although the legislation misspelled Tori Jo's name, the identity of the baby who inspired the document was not in question.

The addition would amend the current PROTECT act by ordering that the national coordinator in consultation with state and local law enforcement agencies to establish minimum standards with the flexibility needed to enable an Amber Alert to be issued without hesitation in the event of another newborn abduction. According to the National Center of Missing and Exploited Children, three out of four of the children who die after being abducted, lose their lives within the first three hours. It was vital to bridge that barrier of time in order to save lives.

On January 24, Senators James Talent of Missouri and Russ Feingold of Wisconsin filed an identical bill in the Senate. Despite the rapid response of these legislators—despite the life-and-death nature of their document—the bill had not passed either house by the one-year anniversary of Bobbie Jo's death and Victoria Jo's abduction. In fact, it had not even reached the floor. It still languished in the judicial committees of both the Senate and the House of Representatives.

Congress had plenty of time in 2005 to play political games and point fingers of blame. They had plenty of time to diddle and fret about gay marriage, pork projects and building walls on our borders to separate our country from another—resurrecting the unwelcome ghost of the Berlin Wall in the land of the free.

The congressmen seemed to have lots of time on their hands, but they could not find the time to address more urgent concerns of the American public. They could not locate the necessary funding to help low-income families pay for heating costs in a year when the price of heating oil and natural gas skyrocketed. Nor could they find the time to deal with the pending health care crisis as the number of uninsured Americans escalated.

And they could not find the time to talk about and take action on the Tory Jo's Loophole bill—a bill that could save the lives of babies across the nation. Tori Jo survived the eight-hour delay in the commencement of the Amber Alert. Although the profile of infant abductors indicated that they would not intentionally harm their victim, there was no guarantee that the next baby taken in a caesarean abduction would be as fortunate as Tori Jo.

Lisa's youngest child, Kayla, spent 2005 rebuilding her life. At Dewey High School in October she was named one of two Sophomore Students of the Month. The faculty made the selection based on the criteria that the recipient was an all-round good student with great attitudes toward the school community and who demonstrated respect for others. Winning this award put Kayla in the running for Student of the Year honors.

Taking a positive legacy from her mother, Kayla made plans to raise her own rat terriers. She owned one spayed female that could not be bred but co-owned a male that could. She was saving money as fast as possible to purchase the dogs she needed to get a breeding business off the ground.

After the Stinnett murder, dog lovers across the country reexamined their lifetime habits. A woman named Heather wrote in an online chat room:

> You know, not only was this a tragedy for the mother and her entire family and community, but it was a real wake-up call for me and Neil. I've driven into the boondocks to pick up dogs from total strangers, or "shelters" that are nothing but a few cyclone fence enclosures and a metal shed. Neil has always thought I was taking too many risks, and I vehemently disagreed. I always felt like I couldn't stop living my life because some nut-job might want to do me harm someday.
>
> But this story really shook me. Partly because it was so heinous, and partly because something similar to this could happen to me or any number of people I know at any time. We've decided to start looking again for a second dog, and he has my promise that I won't go alone, and I will always leave directions and contact information for people I'm meeting even if I know them.

In the rat terrier communities, Bobbie Jo's death led to sorrow, paranoia and conflict. Jason Dawson would no longer allow anyone to come to his home to look at puppies unless he was there. He would not take a risk with his wife or children.

Pat Kennedy no longer handed out maps to her home-based kennel. She would not let people drop by on their own timetable. She made rigid appointments and guarded her address with care. It was more than just Bobbie Jo's death that drove her vigilance. She read a story about a rat terrier litter stolen from another breeder's yard—every puppy gone except for one who had burrowed under a blanket and gone unseen by the puppy thief. Pat put padlocks on her gates and dreamed of a safer world.

Dyanne Siktar remarked in a chat room that none of them should post personal information like the news of a pregnancy online. That earned her a lot of grief. She was slammed by one emailer after another. Yet, law enforcement endorsed the truth of her statement. Sheriff Espey said, "Everyone we interviewed said what a good person Bobbie Jo was. Her only mistake was to put a photo of herself pregnant on the Internet."

35

Rumors swirled around Nodaway County in the summer of 2005 that Zeb Stinnett was about to remarry. A member of the Stinnett clan confirmed that his live-in babysitter Terri was his new fiancée. Hand in hand with that story was another: Zeb and his family were putting up blockades to limit Becky Harper's time with Bobbie Jo's baby.

"It's Zeb this and Zeb that," one woman said, "but nothing is ever said about Becky. Sure, Zeb lost his wife of two years, but Bobbie Jo's mother lost her only daughter and her only grandchild was stolen. What about her? What about Becky's pain? Why do they make it so hard for her to see her granddaughter?"

In late July, Becky filed a petition in Holt County Court requesting more visitation with her grandchild. Zeb responded to the court in August saying that he'd restricted contact with the baby because of Becky's "bizarre" behavior.

He claimed she broke into his home and stole a number of items.

Becky admitted to entering his home—but it was not a break-in, she had a key. She also acknowledged taking articles from the home, but all she removed were items belonging to Bobbie Jo that were given to her by her maternal grandmother. Becky did not want Terri—or anyone Zeb married—laying claim to them. "I want my granddaughter to have this stuff," she said. She just wanted to keep these special items secure for Tori Jo until she was older.

Another bone of contention between Zeb and Becky concerned what information Tori Jo should know about her mother's death. In his petition, Zeb insisted that Becky should never talk to Tori Jo about "any events concerning the death and demise of her natural mother." Becky said that learning a distorted version of the truth from mocking classmates would be a cruel, cold way for any child to learn about her mother's fate.

Becky insisted that she would always be responsible and age-appropriate with anything she told her granddaughter. "Later on, somebody is going to tell her. I hope it's him," she said referring to Zeb. "I hope he tells her before she goes to school."

The possibility of Zeb's marriage was an incendiary element coursing beneath the surface of the interaction between Zeb and Becky. If Zeb did marry Terri and Terri adopted Tori Jo, Becky's rights as a grandparent—as limited as they were—would instantly cease altogether, according to current law in Missouri. This fact sent chills up the spine of every loving grandparent who heard it.

Cheryl Huston and Carla Wetzel planned a remembrance service on the one-year anniversary of Bobbie Jo's death and Tori Jo's birth—Friday, December 16, 2005. They wanted to gather everyone next to the brick memorial built to Bobbie Jo's memory in the park in Skidmore. "The entire community

watched Becky grow up and watched Bobbie Jo grow up. It's
good to gather together to support Becky and remember that
Bobbie Jo lived," Cheryl said.

The press release for the event announced three reasons
for the gathering:

> A primary purpose of the event is to remember Bobbie
> Jo Stinnett. It is being held by friends of the family and
> by caring members of her community. It is being held in
> support of her family, in an effort to let them know we
> care about them.
>
> A secondary purpose of the event is to raise aware-
> ness of legislation regarding Tori's Loophole in the Am-
> ber Alert. A final purpose of this event is to bring further
> awareness to restrictions on grandparents' rights of visi-
> tation in Missouri. The maternal grandmother is cur-
> rently limited in visitation.

"Limited visitation" was as officious and cold a phrase
as could be imagined under these circumstances. Becky
Harper's grief was a harsh wound that went deep. She carried Bobbie Jo in her womb for nine months. She raised
her, nurtured her, loved her for all 23 years of her life. Lim-
iting her visitation seemed to be an act of heartlessness and
insensitivity—if not downright cruelty. Two weeks before
Tori Jo's first birthday, Becky told reporter Kathryn Lister:
"Victoria doesn't take the place of my daughter, but she is a
comfort. When she smiles it eases the pain."

The standing of grandparents' rights in Missouri as well
as in most other states seemed on the surface to be a denial
of the bond between grandchild and grandparent. In reality,
though, the issue was far more complex.

In 1965, grandparents' rights were a newly recognized legal concept. For the three decades after that year, the acknow-
ledgment of these rights expanded as state legislators adopted
laws to protect the visitation rights with grandchildren.

Then the courts reversed the trend—finding these laws in

many states to be unconstitutional because they limited the rights of the parents. Even the common standard of decisions based on "the best interests of the child" was overturned in four different states.

The challenges to the law arose from the adversarial nature of divorce itself. Some grandparents used the children as pawns to get back at a former in-law. Their self-centered actions caused a backlash that created a hardship for every loving grandparent whose sole motivation was to maintain contact with their grandchildren.

Cheryl and Carla realized that broadening the rights of all grandparents could open the door to future abuse. However, they advocated an amendment to protect the rights of a grandparent when a child's parent was deceased. The importance of that family link in that situation should be recognized—the added dimension of that bond should be enhanced, not erased.

The evening of the remembrance service was bitter cold—the temperature was 19 degrees and falling. A full moon smiled down on Skidmore and not a single cloud drifted by to obscure the stars. Red and white strands of Christmas icicle lights glittered on the gazebo. Flickering candles circled the memorial to Bobbie Jo, and one lone candle shone bright at the tree planted in memory of Wendy Gillenwater. As people approached the park, Carla and Cheryl offered lit candles to everyone who arrived.

Carla emceed the service, introducing each speaker to the crowd of one hundred shivering souls gathered that night. At 7 P.M., the remembrance opened with a prayer. The first speaker to address the crowd was Cheryl Huston: "I spent hours trying to come up with just the right things to say tonight," she said. Then she crinkled up the pages of her prepared statement and tossed them aside and spoke from her heart. "Nothing I say up here is going to do the one thing that would make Becky feel better, and that is to give her back Bobbie Jo."

Cheryl talked about the closeness between Bobbie Jo and Becky, shared her memories of the little girl who was so full of life, and voiced the hope that Bobbie Jo's life would be remembered. "She didn't just die tragically and her pictures flashed in the papers. She lived, loved horses, loved dogs, she adopted everything with a fuzzy face."

Then Cheryl turned the crowd's focus to the crime itself. "One year ago, a woman from Kansas came here to our community and from that point on, all she did was take. She took Bobbie Jo's life. She caused all of this heartache and destroyed so many lives to cover up the web of lies she had woven for months."

Cheryl wrapped up her comments by talking about the importance of grandparents to children, particularly in the case of a murdered parent, and urged everyone to write letters to their state representatives. She advocated for the passage of the proposed Tory Jo's Loophole amendment to the Amber Alert law.

After a few words from a spokesman from the office of United States Representative Sam Graves, Sheriff Ben Espey addressed the candlelit group. He thanked the media for the role they played in the recovery of Tori Jo and thanked the other members of law enforcement who were present at the service that night. "This shows respect for the family. This community has been labeled as a bad community, and it's not. This murder was a freak thing that shouldn't have happened. But the good news is that little baby survived and how everyone has pulled together."

When asked if he was permitted to visit Tori Jo, he said, "I pretty much have an open-door policy to see her whenever I want."

Many in the crowd were glad to see that Zeb acknowledged his debt of gratitude to Sheriff Espey by allowing him to see the little girl. At the same time, they could not understand why this same freedom was not granted to the mother of his wife, Bobbie Jo.

Reverend Hamon followed Sheriff Espey and continued

the theme of togetherness. He recalled how the country pulled together in the aftermath of the attack on Pearl Harbor and after the terrorist strike on September 11, 2001. He drew a parallel to those incidents and recent events. "And I saw the same thing a year ago. When tragedy strikes, you can fall apart, roll over and play dead, or you can rise to the occasion. I just thank God that we can share together as members of a community such as we have here. Tragedy comes, but we don't have to be defeated by it." He then closed the service by leading everyone in prayer.

The gathering moved into the Newton Community Hall—former home of Mom's Café and the backdrop for Ken McElroy's fatal drama—to share memories and get shelter from the cold and the wind. Some present expressed disappointment that Tori Jo was not there. Others responded to their complaints with common sense—it was just too cold a night to be taking a baby outside at all.

But everyone agreed on one thing—Zeb Stinnett's absence was conspicuous. Most of the folks there knew Zeb. They knew he was an introvert—but still his absence was unsettling. In honor of his wife's memory, they thought, he should have set aside his personal aversion to public appearances and attended her remembrance service. Some even wondered out loud if he really cared—if he really missed Bobbie Jo.

The next day, Becky Harper rose happy and exuberant. Friday night was a bittersweet catharsis. Today was the one day per month that she was allowed to spend with her granddaughter Tori Jo. She'd be able to hold and play with her little granddaughter all day long. Then the phone rang. It was Zeb. He cancelled the scheduled visitation. He claimed Tori Jo was sick.

Despair and grief washed over Becky, drowning all the joy and anticipation she felt when she woke up that morning.

36

In the last week of 2005, Lisa Montgomery's defense attorneys filed a motion in federal court on her behalf:

Capital cases are difficult no matter what—we recognize the need to move forward but despite our best efforts to date, we cannot provide competent representation under the current scheduling order. The necessary investigation, motion practice, discovery and defense scientific testing simply cannot be accomplished without additional time.

To assist the Court and government counsel in appreciating the critical need for this continuance and to demonstrate that this request is not the result of procrastination by defense counsel, this motion will outline numerous stumbling blocks to an April 2006 trial date and the general areas in which extensive work remains to be accomplished.

They argued that

> capital cases are fundamentally different than any
> other criminal case not only in the severity of the po-
> tential penalty but in the nature of the evidence and
> the information which must be developed. Sensitive
> facts need to be disclosed to members of the defense
> team who are essential strangers to the defendant.
> This takes months. Then evaluation by relevant ex-
> perts must follow. It is an incrementally slow process.
>
> Without adequate time to develop the relationship
> of trust required for effective representation in a cap-
> ital case, counsel may never learn or be able to pres-
> ent the most crucial facts about the defendant, facts
> without which any possible understanding of her ac-
> tions is impossible.

The lawyers complained at length about the failure of the
prosecution to provide all the required documents:

> While the government has provided and continues to
> provide, substantial discovery in this case, to date
> neither of the provisions of the scheduling Order have
> been completely complied with by the government.
> There are several items such as documents, film, com-
> puter disks and a tape of a recorded conversation of
> the defendant on January 10, 2005, that have not
> been produced. Government DNA testing is ongoing.
> The government has not yet produced a "bit by bit"
> image of the hard drives of computers seized by the
> government during investigation of this case, includ-
> ing a computer seized from Mrs. Montgomery.

The attorneys also insisted that they needed more time to
conduct their own DNA tests.

What seemed to be their strongest argument for a delay of

trial was the prosecution's belated filing of the formal notice
to seek the death penalty:

> *The scheduling order, in envisioning trial in April*
> *2006, mandated that any notice of intent to seek the*
> *death penalty be filed by September 16, 2005. The*
> *government did not file that notice until two months*
> *later on November 16, 2005. Essentially, the govern-*
> *ment took 11 months to make the decision as to*
> *whether or not to seek the death penalty in this case*
> *and expects the defendant to be prepared to meet that*
> *notice in 5 months. This is simply not enough time.*

The defense, however, was not requesting an additional
sixty days to prepare to compensate for the two-month delay caused by the prosecution—nor were they reverting to
their previous request for an August 2006 date. They wanted
more—much more. They requested a commencement of trial
in February 2007.

The prosecution filed their response to the defense's delay request on January 10, 2006:

> *The United States opposes the request of the defen-*
> *dant to continue her trial to February 2007. The*
> *above case has been specially set for jury trial before*
> *this Court since February 2005. At that time, this*
> *Court advised counsel that the parties should prepare*
> *for trial to being on April 24, 2006. The United States*
> *stands ready to proceed on that date and further sug-*
> *gests there is more than adequate time remaining be-*
> *fore trial for defense counsel to be prepared to meet*
> *their constitutional obligations to provide a sufficient*
> *defense for the defendant.*

They objected to the defense allegation that they were slow
to provide discovery. To date, they asserted that they had given

2,282 **pages** of documentation to their counterparts—all but 145 pages of which were provided before the end of May.

> *The remaining few items of discovery were only recently requested by defense counsel and will be provided in the near future. It should be noted, however, that the items only recently requested by defense counsel on November 30 have been available to defense counsel for review since the spring of 2005 when government counsel invited defense counsel to review the evidence at the FBI at anytime.*

In the matter of the defense's need for additional time for DNA testing, the prosecutor's response was blunt:

> *Although it has been a year since the murder of Bobbie Jo Stinnett, defense counsel still have not requested to have independent testing performed by its own experts on any of the items seized in this investigation by law enforcement authorities. The United States suggests that because of the defendant's confession and the overwhelming weight of the evidence found in the trunk of the defendant's automobile, on her person, and in her home, it is obvious why defense counsel has not requested independent testing.*

They also placed the blame for the delay in providing computer evidence squarely on defense. They claimed Lisa's attorneys created obstacles to the transmission of that material by insisting on specific formats for that delivery. On the matter of the late filing of the *Notice to Seek the Death Penalty,* the prosecution argued that the defense had known for more than a year that the prospect was likely.

The state pointed yet another finger of blame at the defense. The legal team was given four possible days to meet with the Department of Justice's Capital Review Committee in Washington, D.C. "Ms. Hunt and Mr. Owen chose the very last date available, that is September 26, 2005 to make their formal mitigation presentation," despite knowing it would delay the death penalty filing.

The prosecution's position was clear:

> *Defendant is represented by three very skilled and experienced defense attorneys and also has revealed in her motion that she has employed three mitigation experts to assist in her pre-trial investigation and defense at trial. It is simply not credible to suggest that these skilled and experienced attorneys cannot be prepared to defend the charges against the defendant when they have already had over a year to begin preparation for the defense of this case and have nearly five additional months before this case is scheduled for trial.*
>
> *Finally, the family members of the murder victim, Bobbie Jo Stinnett have painfully awaited for the trial of this case and justice dictates . . . that this Court enter an order denying the defendant's motion.*

The judge did not give the defense a February 2007 date as they requested, but he did give them an additional six months. He scheduled a commencement date of October 23, 2006.

Now the decision was in the hands of the judge. The trial was expected to last four weeks from selection of the jury to the delivery of Lisa Montgomery's sentence.

37

As Tori Jo approached her first birthday and her second Christmas, she was an exuberant, chubby baby with the same big eyes her mother had when she was 1 year old. She crawled at high speed, but toddled awkwardly when she tried to walk.

She jabbered away nonstop most of the time she was awake. Just like her mother at that age, the hair on her head was still very sparse.

If only Bobbie Jo could see her now.

AFTERWORD

Acts of evil befall people every single day. Most of us, though, feel snug and secure in our common sense and our ability to judge the people around us. When we learn of great evil committed by history's villains like Hitler, Stalin and Pol Pot, we remain rooted in our personal sense of comfort and security. However, when it's the guy next door or the woman who cleans your teeth at the dental office or the man who repairs your car, the full impact of the ordinariness of evil hits us hard. After the fact, we can look back on the tracks of that person's life and see the warning signs with vivid clarity—but either no one saw them in real time or if they did, were not able or willing to divine their true meaning.

To keep ourselves covered in a mantle of security, we often blame those close to the perpetrator for being stupid or blind or in denial. Deep down, we should know, though, we are shirking from a truth too painful and frightening to face.

We, too, would have been just as oblivious if that ordinary, insidious evil had invaded our lives.

We have evolved in the past century from a society where involuntary commitment to mental institutions was an easy thing—and easily abused by those with a desire for revenge, a wish to hide away a family embarrassment or a need to ostracize someone who did not conform to society's norms. Now, we have a society where commitment or any form of forced therapy or medication is not possible unless the individual harms another or himself. If Judy had been able to commit her daughter Lisa in 2004 when she tried, Bobbie Jo Stinnett might still be alive today.

Is there a standard for commitment in between the two extremes? Is there some way we can act *before* the damage is done? Is there a way we can protect the most vulnerable members in our society—the children, the elderly, the pregnant women—without compromising the civil liberties of us all? There are no easy answers in the challenge of safety versus liberty—in the inevitability that freedom always implies risk.

Every single week in this country, two pregnant women are murdered, making homicide one of the leading causes of death during pregnancy, according to the Center for Disease Control. For a long time, statistics on traumatic deaths as a pregnancy-related phenomenon were overlooked. Researchers had viewed only medical complications and existing health problems as being pregnancy-related.

A fresh review of records, in a number of states, has opened the door to an alarming truth. Thirty-eight percent of pregnant women who died in Washington, D.C., were murdered. Twenty percent of pregnancy deaths in Maryland were caused by homicide. In North Carolina, thirteen percent of deaths were caused by intentional violence. In New York City and Chicago, the overwhelming majority of pregnant women who died of trauma were victims of homicide.

Many states have changed their death certificates. They added a place to indicate whether or not the woman was pregnant when she died. This alteration makes tracking pregnancy-related murders and medical deaths an easier and more accurate task.

Most of the pregnant women whose cause of death is homicide are victims of domestic abuse at the hands of an intimate male partner. Typically, these acts of violence are motivated by a desire to control the woman and to eliminate an unwelcome burden or change in lifestyle for the men.

The need to control is the common thread running between the murders of pregnant women by a male partner and the same crime committed by a woman. The female killers, though, usually do not know their victim very well. A woman like this targets her victim at random in a narcissistic urge to satisfy her own needs without any regard for anyone who stands in her way.

"Female killers who murder pregnant women to steal their babies are not despairing over failed attempts at pregnancy or a recent miscarriage," said criminal profiler Pat Brown. "In fact, they may have lied to family and friends about being pregnant or about losing a child through miscarriage or misfortune.

"They are psychopaths who love the power and attention associated with motherhood, but they don't love the child that true motherhood brings. This kind of woman will only desire a child in order to manipulate others and to bring attention to herself. Should that child stop serving her purposes, she may abandon the child or even kill it. The very act of slaughtering a pregnant woman for her baby negates any possibility that the perpetrator has the capacity to love and care for other human beings. This kind of woman is—to put it simply, without any fancy psychological label—nothing but a cold-blooded killer."

Is there any way a pregnant woman can protect herself from this kind of random attack?[2] There are more than 4.2 million births in this country every year. In 2005, there were

---

[2] If you are expecting a child, visit the website of the National Center for Missing and Exploited Children, www.missingkids.com and download a copy of *What Parents Need to Know*, a list of safety tips for expectant parents, or call 1-800-THE LOST (1-800-843-5678) for free prevention tips or to report any information related to any missing child.

only four infant abductions—not one of them a successful abduction by cesarean section. Statistically, the risk factor for any woman is nonexistent. But statistics do not tell the whole story.

It is a crime that evokes extreme emotion. It devastates the extended family of the victim and carries with it a heavy negative impact on the whole community where the crime occurred.

Its impact casts an even broader net generating a high level of national attention that sends ripples of fear across the nation. This wide-flung focus puts intense pressure on investigators who, in all likelihood, have no experience with this type of predator.

Law enforcement is familiar with criminals whose motivation is money, sex or revenge. Those motives, however, have nothing to do with the crime of infant abduction. According to the National Center for Missing and Exploited Children, the abductor is "desperate to bask in the rapture of baby love—to feel adored and needed." The typical perpetrator "truly believes she is about to give birth and she fully expects everyone to accept the reality she has attempted to create."

"Infant abductors want what they want when they want it. They don't care about who they step on to get there," said Cathy Nahirny at the Center. "If you are standing in their way, they will run you over without a blink of an eye and leave you to die on the pavement while they pursue their all-consuming goal."

Investigators are used to suspects with long rap sheets. But in the case of these abductions, the kidnapper usually does not have a criminal record at all. If she does have any record, it is for minor, nonviolent crimes like shoplifting or check kiting.

"Infant abductions are usually carried out by women who are not criminally sophisticated," according to a September 1995 *FBI Law Enforcement Bulletin*. "However, the women demonstrate an ability to plan the abduction, convincingly play a role . . . and resort to deadly force if necessary. Most of these women are living a lie—before, during and after the abduction, many have faked a pregnancy, which eventually forces them into a corner. They feel they have no choice but to produce a child by any means necessary. Indeed, infant abductions are the desperate acts of desperate women. As one infant abductor put it, 'I began getting really desperate trying to figure out what I was gonna do—how I was gonna find someone to give me their baby—now.' "

It has been said that Bobbie Jo's mistake was to put a picture of herself in an obvious state of pregnancy on the Internet. But is pregnancy something a woman needs to hide? That shrouding of personal information is not far from the days when even married women were confined to home—banished from public—when they were "in the family way"—as if pregnancy were a source of shame.

Bobbie Jo Stinnett was excited about the upcoming birth of her baby. Her pregnancy was a life-altering, life-affirming period in her life. Even for a quiet, reserved person like Bobbie Jo, the anticipation was too exquisite not to share. She should have been able to do so without risk. Today, she should be reveling in the joys and struggling with the challenges of motherhood.

Instead, Bobbie Jo never saw her daughter, Victoria Jo. And Victoria Jo never felt her mother's arms wrap around her or felt the warmth of the intense love that powered her mother's smile.

All because Lisa Montgomery wanted a child and she would not allow anyone to stop her in her quest—not even the life of a lovely small-town woman who was known for her kindness and empathy. The town Montgomery chose for her act of violence was Skidmore—a place already ravaged by a tragic and violent past. A town many say is cursed by the day that its citizens took the law into their own hands and murdered the town bully in cold blood in broad daylight in the busiest intersection for miles.

In my travels through northwest Missouri, I traversed mile after mile of bucolic countryside. I entered many little towns and exchanged a fortune in smiles. But in Skidmore the peace and friendliness—as ordinary in small-town America as fast talk in a big city—sunk into a quagmire of distrust and suspicion.

The moment my foot stretched out of my car, I felt the walls rise and shut me out. A bulky man blocked my entry into a convenience store at Newton's corner. A sour, tired blonde shooed me out of a bar and restaurant nearby. I felt the searing stare of hostile eyes on my back as I stood before the brick memorial erected in Bobbie Jo's memory. When I knocked on doors—with one remarkable, hospitable exception—I was ignored. Although I knew someone was at home, I waited on silent doorsteps in front of doors that did not open. The houses themselves seemed to be holding their collective breath until I left town.

The citizens of many small towns are wary of strangers. But in Skidmore, it went beyond wariness into a simmering paranoia. The folks in Skidmore often express anger and resentment that reporters always bring up Ken McElroy whenever they report anything in Skidmore. Cheryl Huston rebuked the *Maryville Daily Forum* for resurrecting that story, but conveniently forgetting to recall Maryville's own claim to shame—the death of Raymond Gunn. "There is more to Skidmore than Ken McElroy," she said.

The residents who lived in the town all their lives don't want to understand the fascination the rest of the world has for the Ken McElroy story. They are numb to the undercurrents that churn up uneasiness in their own neighborhoods.

As I visited their town, though, I felt the vengeful ghost of Ken McElroy walking the weary streets of Skidmore. I heard him laugh at the isolation and fears of the townspeople—delighted with the thought that he was the root cause of their alienation from the world. And I knew that Ken McElroy had won.